Practices
of
Award-Winning
SECONDARY SCHOOL
Principals

*To school principals and educators everywhere
who are committed to providing an excellent,
equitable education for every child, every day.*

SANDRA
HARRIS

Best
Practices
of
Award-
Winning

SECONDARY SCHOOL

Principals

A Joint Publication

NATIONAL ASSOCIATION
OF SECONDARY SCHOOL
PRINCIPALS

CORWIN
PRESS

FOREWORD BY GERALD N. TIROZZI,
EXECUTIVE DIRECTOR, NATIONAL ASSOCIATION
OF SECONDARY SCHOOL PRINCIPALS

CORWIN PRESS
A SAGE Publications Company
Thousand Oaks, California

For information:

Corwin Press
A Sage Publications Company
2455 Teller Road
Thousand Oaks, California 91320
www.corwinpress.com

Sage Publications Ltd.
1 Oliver's Yard
55 City Road
London EC1Y 1SP
United Kingdom

Sage Publications India Pvt. Ltd.
B-42, Panchsheel Enclave
Post Box 4109
New Delhi 110 017 India

Printed in the United States of America

Library of Congress Cataloging-in-Publication Data

Harris, Sandra.
Best practices of award-winning secondary school principals / Sandra Harris.
    p. cm.
Includes bibliographical references and index.
ISBN 1-4129-2504-5 (cloth)—ISBN 1-4129-2505-3 (pbk.)
    1. High school principals—United States—Case studies. 2. High schools—United States—Administration—Case studies. 3. School improvement programs—United States—Case studies. 4. Educational leadership—United States—Case studies. I. Title.
LB2831.92.H3617 2006
373.12′012—dc22   2005032751

This book is printed on acid-free paper.

06 07 08 09 10   10 9 8 7 6 5 4 3 2 1

Acquisitions Editor:	Elizabeth Brenkus
Editorial Assistant:	Desirée Enayati
Production Editor:	Laureen A. Shea
Copy Editor:	Julie Gwin
Typesetter:	C&M Digitals (P) Ltd.
Proofreader:	Libby Larson
Indexer:	Pamela Van Huss
Cover Designer:	Rose Storey

Contents

Foreword

The No Child Left Behind Act opened a new chapter in U.S. education. The value of its provisions has sparked lively debate for the past several years, but an undisputable reality of the law is the unwavering focus on *schoolwide* success. It's no longer enough to expect that only particular demographics—usually in particular classes—will achieve. Rather, high achievement must become the expectation of *every* student in *every* classroom. Only the principal's purview is sufficiently broad to ensure such schoolwide success.

And so there's never been a better time to consider, as Sandy Harris does in this book, the practices that make principals effective. Now more than ever, what the principal does matters. While much of the literature and research on principal effectiveness over the past decade has offered a bird's-eye view of principal practice, Harris lets us see principal practice at ground level and through the eyes of those who fight the fight every day.

The practices highlighted in this book, each possessed of its own stand-alone value, reflect the wide range of responsibilities secondary school principals assume daily, and the volume of tasks can be enough—sadly, often *is* enough—to deter good candidates from entering the profession. Yet, amid an avalanche of tasks, these principals' voices reveal a fulfillment that eclipses any frustration. We're grateful for the contributions these men and women make each day in their work to their schools and to the profession of the principalship.

—Gerald N. Tirozzi
Executive Director
National Association of Secondary School Principals

Acknowledgments

I wanted to write a book for Corwin Press, so for several years, Robb Clouse and I visited back and forth trying to find just the right topic. Then one day, three years ago, in February 2003, as I was attending an education conference in San Francisco, Robb stopped me in the hall to say that he had just the topic for me: a book on best practices of award-winning principals. I jumped at the opportunity and said, "Yes!"

Writing about best practices of award-winning principals was a great idea. I couldn't wait to start. We divided the project into an elementary school book and a secondary school book. I was reminded during the process of gathering best practices that principals are the most generous, giving, and warm folks you can meet, but they are also incredibly and consistently busy! In July 2004, *Best Practices of Award-Winning Elementary School Principals* (Corwin Press) was completed, and it was released in February 2005.

Beginning the work on this book, *Best Practices of Award-Winning Secondary School Principals*, again reminded me that there is no one busier than a secondary school principal! It has been worth the wait, I hope for readers as well, to bring this book to fruition, for this book has more than 100 best practices that will encourage and help principals all over the world.

I would like to acknowledge the following people, who deserve an award for their help in completing this project:

To Lizzie Brenkus, Corwin Press editor, thank you for your insightful communication and encouragement.

To Candice Ling and Desirée Enayati, editorial assistants at Corwin Press, thank you for your patience.

Reviewers, thank you for your critical suggestions to improve this manuscript.

To Robb Clouse and all the people at Corwin Press who had a part in this project, thank you!

To April Jones and Amanda Jones, doctoral students and graduate assistants in the Lamar University doctoral program in educational leadership, thank you! If it had not been for your support and help, I would still be working on this project.

But most of all, to the busy secondary school principals who submitted their best practice ideas: Thank you!

About the Author

 **Sandra Harris** is associate professor and director of the Center for Doctoral Studies in Educational Leadership at Lamar University in Beaumont, Texas, where she teaches classes in social justice and applied research and other administrator preparation courses. Formerly, she served as a teacher, principal, and superintendent in public and private schools. Her scholarship agenda includes administrator preparation, K–12 peer harassment, and building relationship-oriented, socially just school environments. She publishes and presents at regional, state, and national conferences on these topics.

About the Contributors

Andy Adams
andyaadams@yahoo.com
Ava Middle School
P.O. Box 338
Ava, Missouri 65608
Web site: http://www.avaschools
   .k12.mo.us/middleschool/
   index.htm
Principal: 10 years
School Population: 475
Grades: 5–8
2004 Gold Star School–Missouri
   Department of Elementary &
   Secondary Education
2004 No Child Left
   Behind (NCLB) National
   Blue Ribbon School

Sheila P. Anderson
sanderso@austinisd.org
Clint Small, Jr. Middle School
4801 Monterey Oaks Blvd.
Austin, Texas 78749
Web site: http://www
   .austinisd.org/schools/
   campus
Principal: 29 years
School Population: 1,080

Grades: 6–8
2003 Texas Recognized School, Small
    Middle School
1998 Texas Exemplary School, Patton
    Elementary
1994–1997 Texas Recognized School,
    Patton Elementary
1993 Texas Successful Schools Award,
    Patton Elementary ($92,000)
1992 Texas School of Excellence,
    Patton Elementary
1991 Governor's Educational
    Excellence Exemplary Performance
    Award, Patton Elementary
1988–1989 Texas Education Agency
    Exceptional Achievement Award,
    Patton Elementary
1990 Project A+ Technology Site,
    Patton Elementary ($1.2 million
    IBM grant)
1990 Keep Austin Beautiful
    1st Place Award for Outdoor
    Learning Center, Patton
    Elementary
1989 U.S. Department of Agriculture
    Take Pride in America
    Commendation, Patton
    Elementary
1986 Austin Adopt-a-School
    Principal of the Year

Diane Baker
dbaker@tularosa.k12.nm.us
Tularosa Middle School
504 First St.
Tularosa, New Mexico 88352
Web site: http://www
    .tularosa.k12.nm.us/
Principal: 10 years
School Population:
    290 students
Grades: 6–8

2003–2004 Middle School Principal
    of the Year
Pinon Recognition from Quality New
    Mexico

Stan Beiner
sbeiner@epsteinatlanta.org
The Epstein School
335 Colewood Way
Atlanta, Georgia 30328
Web site: http://www.epstein
    atlanta.org
Head of School: 9 years
School Population: 685 students
Grades: Pre-K–8
2004 NCLB Blue Ribbon School
Outstanding Alumni Award–
    University of Judaism
2003 Recognized as one of Atlanta's
    best independent schools—
    Atlanta Magazine

Marla S. Brady
mlee@fau.edu
A.D. Henderson University School
Florida Atlantic University High
    School
777 Glades Road
Boca Raton, Florida 33431
Web site: http://www.adhus.fau
    .edu/index.html
Principal: 10 years
School Population: 650 students
Grades: K–8
2004–2005 Florida "A" rated school
2005 NCLB Blue Ribbon School

Tim Brady
Bradyt@usd231.com
Wheatridge Middle School
318 East Washington
Gardner, Kansas 66030

Web site: http://www.usd231.com
Principal: 6 years
School Population: 520 students
Grades: 7–8
2004 Kansas Middle School Principal
of the Year
1987 Middle School Director of the
Year
Kindest Kansas Citian Nominee
State Standard of Excellence in
Reading
Goals 2000 Grant Recipient
Kansas Association of Middle Level
Educators (KAMLE) Oasis School
Award
KAMLE Focus School Award
Kansas City Youth Alliance–School of
Service Award

Stewart Carey
scarey@westfieldnjk12.com
Roosevelt Intermediate School
301 Clark Street
Westfield, New Jersey 07090
Web site: http://www.westfield
njk12.org/education/school/
Principal: 2 years
School Population: 731 students
Grades: 6–8
2003–2004 NCLB Blue Ribbon School
(When Roosevelt was recognized
as a Blue Ribbon School, Kenneth
Shulack was principal. Carey was
assistant principal in Westfield
District.)
2003–2004 Honored by the State of
New Jersey as a Blue Ribbon
School

Becke Cleaver
BCleaver@Clark.k12.ky.us
Conkwright Middle School
360 Mt. Sterling Road

Winchester, Kentucky 40391
Web site: http://www.clark
.k12.ky.us/conkm
Principal: 14 years
School Population: 540 students
Grades: 6–8
2003 Kentucky Middle School
Principal of the Year
1993 Leadership Kentucky
1992 University of Kentucky College
of Education Hall of Fame
1992 7th District Parent/Teacher
Association Principal of the Year
1988 Stella Edwards Kentucky Special
Education Teacher of the Year
1987 Special Education Teacher of the
Year, Fayette County Schools

Brent Curtice
Fishbc007@yahoo.com
Paonia High School
846 Grand Avenue
Paonia, Colorado 81428
Web site: http://www.deltaschools
.com/Paonia_7_12/
Principal: 10 years
School Population: 286 students
Grades: 9–12
2004 MetLife/NASSP Colorado High
School Principal of the Year
State Sportsmanship Award
Many activity awards

Susan G. Curtis
Susanc1@wcs.edu
Grassland Middle School
2390 Hillsboro Road
Franklin, Tennessee 37069
Web site: http://www.wcs
.edu/gms/
Principal: 1 year
School Population: 975 students
2004 NCLB Blue Ribbon School

Evelyn Ennsmann
EENNSMANN@dupage88.net
Willowbrook High School
1250 S. Ardmore
Villa Park, Illinois 60181
Web site: http://hsdist88.dupage
.k12.il.us/wbhs/
Principal: 7 years
School Population:
2,300 students
Grades: 9–12
2004 MetLife/NASSP Illinois High
School Principal of the Year
Regional Principal of the Year in
Indiana

Anthony Ferreira
aferreira@dighton-rehoboth
regional.k12.ma.us
Dorothy Beckwith
Middle School
330R Winthrop Street
Rehoboth, Massachusetts 01769
Web site: http://drregional.org/
SUPER/home.html
Principal: 21 years
School Population: 650 students
Grades: 5–8
2003 MetLife/NASSP Massachusetts
Principal of the Year

Kevin Fillgrove
K_fillgrove@easd.k12.pa.us
Ephrata Middle School
957 Hammon Avenue
Ephrata, Pennsylvania 17522
Web site: http://www.easd.k12.pa
.us/ems/
Principal: 14 years
School Population: 950 students
Grades: 6–8
2004 MetLife/NASSP Pennsylvania
Principal of the Year

2003 American Red Cross
Philanthropist of the Year
2002 National Blue Ribbon

Kevin R. Fitzgerald
Kevin.fitzgerald@cr.k12.de.us
Caesar Rodney High School
239 Old North Road
Camden, Delaware 19934
Web site: http://www.k12.de
.us/crhs
Principal: 8 years
School Population: 1,800 students
Grades: 9–12
2004 University of Delaware's
Commitment to Educational
Excellence Award
NCLB Superior rating every year;
one of two Delaware high schools
to be recognized for two
consecutive years
2004 Siemans' Foundation recognized
Caesar Rodney for its advanced
placement programs
2004 President of Delaware Secondary
School Principal's Association
2002 Delaware State Principal of the
Year
1998 School recognized as Superstar
in Education by the Chamber of
Commerce

Tommy Floyd
Tommy.floyd@education.ky.gov
Somerset High School
301 College Street
Somerset, Kentucky 42501
Web site: http://www.somerset
.k12.ky.us/
Principal: 7 years
School Population: 500+ students
2004 MetLife/NASSP Kentucky
School Principal of the Year

2004 Kentucky Administrator
of the Year
The high school continually is placed
in the top 30 high schools in the
state.
Floyd is currently a Highly Skilled
Educator for the Kentucky
Department of Education.

Dorothy Garrison-Wade
Dorothy.garrison-wade@cudenver
.edu
Campus Box 106, P.O. Box 173364
Denver, Colorado 80521
Trask Middle School
Wilmington, North Carolina 28405
Web site: http://www.nhcs.k12.nc
.us/trask
Lakeside High School
Wilmington, North Carolina 28405
Web site: http://www.nhcs.k12.nc
.us/lakeside
Principal: 3 years
School Population: middle school,
1,000 students; high school,
211 students
Grades: middle school, 6–8; high
school, 6–12
2001–2002 New Hanover County
Principal of the Year
2001–2002 First Union National
Bank/Ben Craig Principal
of the Year
1998 University of North
Carolina–Chapel Hill Assistant
Principal Executive Program
Outstanding School Improvement
Plan Award
Garrison-Wade is currently an
assistant professor at the
University of Colorado at Denver
and Health Sciences.

Lyman Goding
Lymangoding@yahoo.com
Plymouth Community Intermediate
School
117 Long Pond Road
Plymouth, Massachusetts 02360
Web site: http://pilgrims.net/
plymouth/schools/pcis/
Principal: 31 years
School Population: 1,450 students
Grades: 6–8
2005 DisneyHand Administrator
Award–Disney Teacher of the
Year Program
2004 Massachusetts Middle School
Principal of the Year
2004 Paul Harris Fellow Award by
International Rotary of
America–Community
Service
2003 Patriotic Employer of
Massachusetts Award–National
Committee for Employer Support
of the Guard and Reserve
2003 Outstanding Professional Award
by National Alliance for Mentally
Ill/Plymouth Area
2002 100 Most Wired Schools—
recognition by *PC Family Magazine*
Goding retired in 2005 after 31 years
as a secondary school principal.
He continues to work with
principals at Bridgewater State
College in Massachusetts and is
active in the Massachusetts
Secondary School Administrator
Association.

Eric Grantz
egrantz@humboldt.k12.ca.us
Jacoby Creek School
1617 Old Arcata Road

Bayside, California 95524-9324
Web site: http://internet.humboldt
.k12.ca.us/jacobycreekschool/
Principal: 13 years
School Population: 422 students
Grades: K–8
2004 NCLB
Blue Ribbon School

Tom Hamilton
THAMILTON@btown.k12.ky.us
Bardstown High School
400 N. 5th St.
Bardstown, Kentucky 40004
Web site: www.btown.k12.ky.us/bhs/
Principal: 13 years
School Population: 500 students
Grades: K–12
2005 MetLife/NASSP Kentucky
Principal of the Year
2004–2005 Kentucky Department of
Education Reward School
2001 National Association of Year
Round Schools School of Merit

Kathleen Genovese Haworth
kathleenhaworth@laurelhall.com
Laurel Hall School
11919 Oxnard Street
North Hollywood, California 91606
Web site: http://www.laurelhall.com
Principal: 8 years
School Population: 570 students
Grades: K–8
2003 Steve Allen Educational
Excellence Award
2003 Nova Southeastern/National
Association of Elementary School
Principals National Fellow
Scholarship
2002 National Distinguished
Principal

Carole Hiltman
cdhiltman@juno.com
Esparto Middle School
26675 Plainfield
Esparto, California 95627
Web site: http://www.espartok12
.org/ms/
Principal: 17 years
School Population: 220 students
Grades: 6–8
2004 NCLB Blue Ribbon School
2004 Region 3 Educator of the Year
Nominee
2003 California Distinguished School
2003 Yolo County Golden Apple
Administrator Award
2003–2004 Title I Achieving School
1991–1992 Solano County
Administrator of the Year
Previous School: Benicia
Middle School (1,400 students)
Title I Achieving School
California Distinguished School
National Blue Ribbon School

Shirley Johnson
E-mail: rbjohns@flex.net
Sam Houston State University
3044 Bentwater Drive West
Montgomery, Texas 77556
Principal: 17 years as principal
School selected as one of
10 Ted Sizer's Coalition of
Essential Schools
1998 Annenberg Fellow
1997 Danforth Fellow
1996 Paul Harris Fellow
1996 Thomson Fellow
1996 Hometown Hero Recognition
1993–1997 Texas High School Mentor
1994–1996 Principal of the Pew
Foundation Five Schools Project

1993 Southwest Houston Woman of 1993
1993 Houston Woman on the Move
1983 Charter Member of the Coalition of Essential Schools

Marla W. McGhee
mmcghee@austin.rr.com
C.D. Fulkes Middle School
Round Rock ISD
4106 Great Plains Drive
Austin, Texas 78735
Web site: http://www.roundrockisd.org/cdfulkes
Principal: 14 years
School population: 1,200 students
Grades: 6–8
2005 Coauthor of *The Principal's Guide to a Powerful Library Media Program* (Linworth Publishing)
2003 Sue German Award for Excellence
1996 Principals' A Honor Roll
1995 One of three national finalists for the Principal in Residence position at the U.S. Department of Education
1994 Texas representative for National Distinguished Principal
1992 U.S. Department of Education Blue Ribbon School
Today, McGhee teaches in the master's and doctoral programs in educational leadership at Texas State University–San Marcos and is codirector of the National Center for School Improvement.

Heath E. Morrison
Heath_E_Morrison@mcpsmd.org
Thomas Stone High School
3785 Leonardtown Road

Waldorf, Maryland 20601
Web site: http://www.ccboe.com/stone/
Principal: 8 years
School Population: 2,100 students
Grades: 9–12
2004 MetLife/NASSP Maryland State Principal of the Year
2003 Washington Post Distinguished Educational Leadership Award
2003 Charles County Principal of the Year
2003 Congressional Citation from Congressman Steny Hoyer
2003 Maryland State Principal of the Year by the Maryland Association of Student Councils
2003 Thomas Stone High School recognized by *Newsweek Magazine* as a top 3% performing school in the nation
2001 Charles County Principal of the Year by Charles County Association of Student Councils

Allan Mucerino
mucerinoa@svusd.k12.ca.us
LaPaz Intermediate School
25151 Pradera Drive
Mission Viejo, California 92691-5210
Web site: http://www.svusd.k12.ca.us/schools/La_Paz/
Principal: 5 years
School Population: 1,280 students
Grades: 7–8
2004 NCLB Blue Ribbon School
2003 California Distinguished School
1999 Principal of the Year (Principal of Ensign Intermediate School in Newport-Mesa Unified School District)

Melinda Reeves
Melinda.reeves@decatur.esc11.net
Decatur High School
1201 W. Thompson
Decatur, Texas 76234
Web site: http://www.decatur
   .esc11.net/campuses/dhs/
   index.html
Principal: 9 years
School Population: 850 students
Grades: 9–12
2004 Blue Ribbon School
Mentor School
National Finalist Teacher of the Year
Texas Teacher of the Year
Regional XI Teacher of the Year

Mark Roherty
mroherty@mtsd.k12.wi.us
Homestead High School
5000 W. Mequon Road
Mequon, Wisconsin 53092
Web site: http://www.mtsd.k12
   .wi.us/
Principal: 15 years
School Population: 1,620 students
Grades: 9–12
2004 NCLB Blue Ribbon School
2003 Martin Family Achievement
   Award
1995 Principal of the Year in Mequon-
   Thiensville School District

Manette Schaller
steveteg@alltel.net
Alief Taylor High School
7555 Howell Sugar Land Road
Houston, Texas 77083
Web site: http://www.alief
   .isd.tenet.edu/taylor/htm
Principal: 17 years
School Population: 2,727 students
Grades: 9–12

2004–2005 Texas Association of
   Secondary School Principals
   Region 4 High School Principal of
   the Year
2004–2005 State Finalist for High
   School Principal of the Year
2001–2002 Texas Education Agency
   Recognized Campus
1998 Lifetime Member of Texas
   Association for Alternative
   Schools–Texas Association for
   Alternative Education
1993 Alief Paraprofessional of the Year

Kristine Servais
kservais@noctrl.edu
Bay View Middle School
2700 Lineville Road
Green Bay, Wisconsin 54313
Web site: http://www.hssd.k12.wi
   .us/bayview
Principal: 8 years
School Population: 900 students
Grades: 6–8
1994 Blue Ribbon School

Daniel Stepenosky
dstepenosky@bhusd.k12.ca.us
Beverly Hills High School
241 Moreno Drive
Beverly Hills, California 90212-3698
http://www.bhhs.beverlyhills
   .k12.ca.us
Principal: 3 years
School Population: 2,200 students
2004 National Blue Ribbon School
2000 National Blue Ribbon School
2003 New American High
   School–California Distinguished
   High School
1999 New American High
   School–California Distinguished
   High School

Marilyn Svaluto
svalutom@sgate.k12.mi.us
Davidson Middle School
15800 Trenton Road
Southgate, Michigan 48195
Web site: http://www.southgate
    schools.com/Schools/davidson
    .htm
Principal: 11 years
School Population: 806 students
Grades: 8–9
2003 MetLife/NASSP Michigan
    Principal of the Year
1991–1992 Southgate Community
    School District Employee of the
    Year
Twice published in NASSP journal
    Principal Leadership

Sharon L. Toriello
toriellos@kinnelon.org
Kinnelon High School
121 Kinnelon Road
Kinnelon, New Jersey 07405
Web site: http://www.kinnelon
    publicschools.org
Principal: 6 years
School Population: 613 students
Grades: 9–12
2004 MetLife/NASSP New Jersey High
    School Principal of the Year

Dana Salles Trevethan
DTrevethan@turlock.k12.ca.us
Turlock High School
1600 E. Canal Drive
Turlock, California 95380
Web site: http://www.turlock
    .k12.ca.us/ths/
Principal: 4 years
School Population: 2,300+ students
Grades: 9–12

2005 Principal Lip Sync Regional
    Championship
2003–2004 Stanislaus County Drug
    Free Award
2003–2004 State and National Future
    Farmers of America
    Championships
2002–2005 Stanislaus County
    Occupational Olympics Large
    School Sweepstakes
2002 Bell Award, California School
    Board Association, High School
    English/Language Arts Reading
    Program

James (Jim) Winston Wells
James.wells@cfisd.net
Thornton Middle School
9802 Keith Harrow Boulevard
Katy, Texas 77449
Web site: http://www.cfisd.net
School Population:
    1,767 students
Grades: 6–8
Cypress Creek High School
9815 Grant Road
Houston, Texas 77070
Web site: http://www.cfisd.net
Principal: 13 years as a principal.
School Population: 2,715 students
Grades: 9–12
1999–2000 National Blue Ribbon
    School of Excellence
Wells is currently in his fourth year as
    principal at Cypress Creek High
    School.

Introduction

> The greatest compliment that was ever paid to me was when
> someone asked me what I thought, and attended to my answer.
> —*Henry David Thoreau*
> *(as cited in Blaydes, 2003, p. 176)*

Being a principal in the 21st century is a challenge. To qualify for the job, principals need to be visionaries, instructional leaders, curriculum specialists, technology experts, disciplinarians, facility managers, budget analysts, community representatives, politicians, counselors, public relations experts, testing gurus, legal analysts, policy writers, and mediators. And don't forget, they need to know something about educating children, too. Along with all of these responsibilities, today's schools are rated from exemplary to unacceptable based on the results of mandated one-size-fits-all standardized tests. Consequently, it seems that nearly every day, the media reports about our failing public schools, and the "blame game" is in full swing as everyone seeks to find fault for failing schools. Many times, principals end up in this "hot seat" when they are told that if a school does not achieve a certain rating, they will be reassigned, if not terminated from the job altogether. To make things even harder, more children than ever before are enrolled in our schools—nearly 48,000,000 students in U.S. public schools and 6,000,000 in our private, independent schools! That is a lot of blame for principals to bear.

Is it possible that in our zeal to educate all of America's children and educate them well, our criticism is out of balance? Is it possible that although our schools have room for improvement, good things are still happening in them? Can it be that we are so busy finding fault with what is not working, we are failing to notice what is working? Maybe Mark Twain was on to something when he quipped, "Schools ain't what they used to be—but they never were" (as cited in Blaydes, 2003, p. 130).

We know that successful school leaders have a strong influence on student achievement as they support and develop effective teachers and as they implement effective organizational processes (Davis, Darling-Hammond, LaPointe, & Meyerson, 2005). Consistently, research for effective schools has found that principals of these schools have common behaviors. For example, they

- are assertive instructional leaders,
- are goal and task oriented,
- delegate responsibility to others,
- communicate high expectations for all,
- define and communicate school policies clearly,
- are visible,
- support good teaching, and
- build strong relationships with parents and the community (Robinson, 1985).

This list identifies much of what effective principals do and often what we look for when identifying strong principals.

Despite what the media would have us believe, you and I know that great principals are leading effective schools throughout our nation. I teach in an educational leadership preparation program, and every day I see and talk with hard-working, effective principals who are leading strong schools for today's children. They are all around us. In addition, every year, organizations such as the National Association of Secondary School Principals (NASSP) and National Association of Elementary School Principals recognize these principals for their successful school leadership.

How do these effective principals know what best practices to use? Many times, they select programs and strategies based on what research has identified as effective. Other times, they choose a strategy based on what they have seen be successful for others, and sometimes, they listen to their own "inner compass" and select practices intuitively based on what they feel their school needs. This book is a qualitative study that asks the question: What best practices are principals who have been recognized for their leadership implementing on their campuses? To identify these strategies, I e-mailed, faxed, telephoned, and wrote letters to secondary school principals who were recognized for their success. I asked them to describe the practices that they attributed to their success and to the success of their school. In other words, what did award-winning principals consider their best practices at their schools?

The 34 principals, representing MetLife/NASSP State Principal award winners, Blue Ribbon Schools award winners, and other recognized principals who contributed best practices to this book lead public and private schools in a variety of settings all across the United States. Their schools represent an array of diverse populations, ethnicities, learning styles, and other differences. Although the practices submitted rarely fit neatly into just one category, and all represented various examples of leadership, I categorized them into the following chapters:

- Leadership
- Shaping Campus Culture
- Communicating for Collaboration
- Curriculum and Instruction
- School Improvement Plans
- Personalizing the Learning Environment for All

Chapter 7 is a compilation of principals' brief words of wisdom, and Chapter 8 is a complete resource of books principals consider "must reads."

At the end of Chapters 1 through 6, I have included a brief summary of the award-winning practices principals shared. By glancing at the practices in each summary box, the reader can get a quick picture of best practices that worked for these principals.

Also at the end of Chapters 1 through 6, I have included questions to encourage reflection. Learning about best practices is important, but the challenge does not end there. For these practices to be implemented in our schools, the next step is reflection. Reflection helps principals think through new ideas and consider how they will work in their school and how they might need to be revised or restructured. This ongoing process contributes to the successful implementation of many of these ideas. As you read through the ideas, consider your own school. Identify areas in which your school is strong and areas in which you are strong. Then, identify areas of weakness. Which ideas in these chapters would be most helpful to your campus? Write these ideas down, then consider how you can implement them in your school. Will they need to be revised to be most effective at your school?

Finally, the chapters conclude with a list of resources to help readers gather extra information about interesting ideas that were mentioned from the Internet.

Of course, it is true that not all schools are doing some things well. Recognizing that, it is our responsibility to improve them. But who should provide that help? One obvious resource is to seek support from the best of the best themselves, those who are recognized as effective principals. The best practices in this book are strategies, programs, ideas, and suggestions from those who have been recognized as award winners. As award-winning principal Lyman Goding told me, "We do not call them 'best practices,' we call them 'successful practices,' because there are so many great and successful ideas." So don't let the title *Best Practices* fool you into thinking that one size fits all! The word *best* suggests that there is only one way, but the principals who contributed to this book submitted a variety of strategies and ideas that have proven successful in their schools. Rarely are these earth-shattering, radical new ideas that lead to a new concept of leadership. Instead, most often, they redirect and refocus us to what is important and what is proven to work. It is our hope that in this collection, principals everywhere will find ideas, strategies, and best practices that will help them be successful in leading their schools to be the best they can be!

Principals sit in the hot seat every day. If they must accept much of the blame when something does not work, they should accept the praise when it does. To the award-winning principals who contributed to this project, thank you for sharing your award-winning best practice ideas.

REFERENCES

Blaydes, J. (2003). *The educator's book of quotes.* Thousand Oaks, CA: Corwin Press.

Davis, S., Darling-Hammond, L., LaPointe, M., & Meyerson, D. (2005). *School leadership study: Developing successful principals.* Stanford, CA: Stanford Educational Leadership Institute.

Robinson, G. E. (1985). *Effective schools research: A guide to school improvement.* Arlington, VA: Educational Research Service.

CHAPTER ONE

Leadership

It has often been said that children are the messages that we send to the future. I believe that school leaders are the guides to those children as they embark on that journey.
—*Brent Davies (2005, p. 9)*

For more than 200 years, the public school, America's primary resource for educating young people, has been led by principals. In the early 1800s, Horace Mann rode on horseback to check on schools; today, principals walk from classroom to classroom with handheld computers to log in their observations. Then, Mann's goal was that public schools would "serve all boys and girls . . . [and] would give each student an equal chance in life" (as cited in Mondale & Patton, 2001, p. 29). Today's successful principals still believe in that same goal, and they have invested their lives in school leadership to give students that opportunity.

The connection between effective principals, effective schools, and leadership is strong. But what does this leadership look like? Although research has identified many different definitions for the term *leadership*, most would generally agree that a leader is seen as the one who points to or shows others the way to a destination or a goal. Leithwood and Jantzi (2005) identified three categories of transformational leadership practices in schools, which include setting directions, developing people, and redesigning the organization. This is not unlike the three categories that Hallinger and Heck (1999) noted in their review of educational leadership—purposes, people, and structures and social systems. Therefore, the leadership role of the principal is to understand how to support teachers, manage the curriculum to promote student learning, and transform schools into effective organizations in which powerful teaching occurs and all students learn (Davis, Darling-Hammond, LaPointe, & Meyerson, 2005). All of this is done today under the glare of an accountability spotlight that seems to be more often interested in naming scapegoats than noting solutions. Being a principal is not a leadership task that just anyone is able to fill.

At the same time, school districts are struggling to attract and retain highly qualified leaders, as nearly 60% of principals will retire, resign, or otherwise leave their positions over the next five years (Peterson, 2002). Tim Brady, an award-winning principal, reminds us that principal leadership can often be found through inner direction to "lead on a larger scale." This is one way that Tim, in his best practice advice, provides encouragement and motivation to all principals and aspiring principals about why anyone would leave the "tranquility" of the classroom for the "turbulence" of the principalship.

When award-winning secondary school principals submitted their best practices in leadership, in general, these practices were consistent with the research on transformational leadership. For example, Sheila Anderson noted that the principal "must know where he or she is going, be well planned and organized, and build meaningful and caring relationships." (Setting direction, redesigning the organization, and developing people—sound familiar?) Other principals used words such as *trust, care, planning, vision,* and *teamwork* when describing best practice leadership behaviors that have helped them become outstanding school leaders with a vision to, as Tommy Floyd said, "put kids first."

This chapter includes a particularly unique perspective on leadership. Kristine Servais, an award-winning principal in 1994, is now an assistant professor at North Central College in Naperville, Illinois. She writes about many of the leadership best practices she implemented at a middle school several years ago and looks at them in retrospect. Now, several years later, this is particularly powerful because many of these same best practices are still contributing to an effective school.

LEADERSHIP ACTIONS THAT BUILD EXEMPLARY SCHOOLS

Sheila P. Anderson
Austin, Texas

I had been an assistant principal for three years when I was appointed to my first principalship. Soon after that appointment, I was asked by an experienced principal if I thought like a principal yet. I responded that I still thought like a teacher. He assured me that I would change, implying that it would be for the better. Yet today, after 29 years as a principal, I still think like a teacher. I simply have a group of older students, my staff. A classroom teacher must know where he or she is going, be well planned and organized, and build meaningful and caring relationships. This is just as true for the principal.

In today's high-stakes world, we know where we are going: toward all children being successful and graduating from high school and beyond. Getting to that goal can be a challenge. There are some simple things that have seemed to pay off in the schools in which I have been principal. One of them has to do with the belief that the school should be organized in a way that supports trust and removes barriers to teachers doing their jobs. In a nutshell, here are the main components:

- *Hire wisely.* Use an interview team, and don't second-guess your gut. Keep looking until you are satisfied. Usually, our team consists of the department head and a teacher from the grade level or team that has the vacancy. We have set questions we ask all interviewees and a questionnaire we ask the person to complete when he or she arrives and before the interview. The questionnaire is one we developed that allows the candidate to share some philosophical and practical background information. We review the district application, resume, written document, and interview responses as we make decisions.
- *Establish a governing body* of teachers who are elected by their peers to serve, rotating this responsibility every two years or so. Expect everyone to serve over time.
- *Build the capacity of that governing body* to emphasize leadership qualities, problem solving, decision making, and communication skills. One of the best things I have done to help me do this is to be a member of the National Staff Development Council (NSDC) and attend their national conference. Robert Garmston and Bruce Wellman (1999) have written a book called *The Adaptive School: A Sourcebook for Developing Collaborative Groups.* It is one of the best resources I know for helping a staff and community work together. The authors present at the NSDC conference and also offer week-long sessions for teams. Any of the major work on change can also be helpful in helping folks understand and work through change.
- *Collaboratively develop clear expectations* regarding teacher performance and school operations.

- *Build trust* by developing the operating budget collaboratively, emphasizing that not everyone can have everything at one time, but over time, everyone can have all they need. (See that they do!)
- *Work with teachers* to have them agree that there will be an open supply room and copying materials will be monitored, but the budget decisions will be based on honesty and need.
- *Organize and train the office staff* so that they are part of the school's vision, serving the teachers and parents as major links in the communication process. We collaboratively develop a written document that outlines major and secondary responsibilities of each office person. This is given to teachers. My secretary acts as office manager and oversees the training and quality control of the office. Service with a smile is expected. We develop phone and personal communication skills and strive to meet the need of the caller on the first try. Everyone understands that we are here to serve children, and we do that by assisting teachers and parents in any way necessary. We also emphasize a team approach to tasks. Much of the office staff's work can be done better by two or three people, so it is common to see them working together to finish a big project. We are also blessed with many parent volunteers. We have written guidelines and training for them as well. I meet monthly with the office staff to see how things are going and to problem solve issues as needed. We also celebrate each person's birthday with goodies and funny cards from all the others. No gifts, just laughs.
- *Train* your secretary to manage your snail mail, e-mail, calendar, and appointments.
- *Use a wide variety of communication strategies* to keep everyone organized and informed (i.e., electronic master calendar, daily calendar sent by e-mail, bulletin board with daily schedule, broadcast e-mail to parents, Web sites for the school and individual teachers).
- *Be visible,* not just in the classrooms, but in the halls and teacher and parent work areas.
- *Know your teachers* like you expect them to know their students, and treat them as you expect them to treat their students. Much has been written about the importance of teachers having respectful relationships with their students. I think that philosophy holds true for principals and their teachers: Listen—this is more important than talking—ask questions that lead to solutions, give feedback that can be used in the learning and growth process of the teacher,

pair a teacher with another teacher who is skilled in the area being addressed, and be truthful without being judgmental.

- *Give teachers feedback* based on where they are, and emphasize the growth they are making toward the school's goals.

- *Know the school's performance data* inside and out, make them public, and set up processes for teachers to work collaboratively to improve their work. In Texas, we get a great deal of state data on our schools. The performance of students is broken down by subgroups similar to No Child Left Behind (NCLB). Our district has provided us with electronic programs that sort and group results by students, teachers, grade, objectives, socioeconomic status, limited English proficiency, ethnicity, and so forth. Being able to produce tables and graphs to help teachers see the patterns and areas of need has been very helpful. Anyone can do this with the use of a spreadsheet, but it is very helpful if school and district data can be dumped into a program, thereby saving the time it takes to manually enter the data. Lightspan and SchoolNet provide such assistance. Our school-wide data are sent home to parents in a report card once a year. Teachers work with bits and pieces of the data throughout the year to guide in lesson planning and student tutoring. By department and objective, teachers review each other's student performance, and high-performing teachers share strategies that seem to significantly improve student learning. I also see that teachers go to staff development that develops their skills as trainers. For example, I have two teachers who are certified trainers for the New Jersey Writing Project.

- *Know the curriculum well,* attend national conferences, and read, read, read so that you are viewed as knowledgeable about change, trends, and innovations.

- *Be a professional developer* with a deep bag of strategies to aid your teachers in learning. It is important to understand and use the processes of setting group norms, brainstorming, using effective meeting structure, resolving conflicts, and knowing change theory. The Dupont Leadership training, along with Garmston and Wellman's (1999) book *The Adaptive School,* have heavily influenced my ability to facilitate groups with these strategies, and I highly recommend them to anyone who leads a school. Probably the technique that has recently aided my teachers the most is KASAB (Knowledge, Attitude, Skill, Aspiration, Behavior). This is a process used to develop effective and measurable staff development created by Linda Munger and Joellen Killion. I developed a spreadsheet from their work that we use in the summer to develop our yearlong staff plan. Once we have decided on a goal, we complete the form by deciding what teachers need to know, what attitudes they need to possess, what skills are necessary for teachers to have, what aspirations must exist, and what behaviors are necessary for the successful attainment of the goal. Once those are identified, we decide what and how much staff development will be necessary to achieve the goal. Here is the table we complete:

Focus	Definition	Teacher	Staff Development Need	When	Where
Knowledge	Conceptual understanding of information, theories, and research				
Attitude	Beliefs about the value of particular information or strategies				
Skill	Strategies and processes to apply knowledge				
Aspiration	Desires or internal motivation to engage in a particular practice				
Behavior	Consistent application of knowledge and skills				
Notes:					

- *Put yourself and your school at the forefront of innovations;* this is a great motivator.
- *Be patient;* good things take a little time.
- *Believe* in your teachers.
- *Believe* in yourself.

Simply stated, this list confirms what research and educational writers have been saying for years. They are right! By the way, my colleague was wrong. I still think like a teacher. I am still a principal. He is no longer in education.

LEADERSHIP: TIM'S TOP 10 TIPS

Tim Brady
Gardner, Kansas

Teachers are the leaders of the classroom. Every child looks toward the teacher for guidance, direction, comfort, and opportunity. Teachers set the tone, manage personalities, discipline, motivate, and even parent.

Teachers are much like athletic coaches. They guide a team of players. There is a beginning and end to the season. The classroom is like the locker room, adorned with inspirational messages and eager players. The season, much like a school year, begins with great enthusiasm and hope. Fundamentals are taught. Improvement is desired. Teamwork is emphasized. Cheerleaders are on the sideline. Injuries occur. There are tests. There are wins and losses. The team owner, called the board of education, judges every move you make. Once the season comes to a close, the players move on. The coach sticks around for another year, promising that next season will be even better.

If you are reading this book, most likely you are a secondary school educator. You have experienced the peaks and valleys of a school year, much like a coach who endures a sports season. Your students are like athletes. These players put you in a positive light. Success feels good because you have contributed to their triumph. Your leadership impacted the life of an adolescent.

The flip side of teaching is that not all of your players achieved the gains you and others had hoped for. Despite your best efforts, some kids fall short of expectations. Exemplary educators begin to evaluate why everyone did not achieve the set goals: What could I have done differently? What "buttons" should have been pushed? Where were the breakdowns during the season? Was the classroom climate conducive for the children to experience success? Was there the necessary support? What went wrong? Where did I fail as a teacher?

As a classroom teacher and coach, I enjoyed every year I worked. I chose to focus on the positive aspects of school life. Each school year had its own personality. The newness in the fall was still able to sustain itself in the spring. My students kept me alert and fresh. I felt this tremendous obligation to dig deep inside myself every class period. I wanted to give my students my best. My efforts constantly led me to instruct, challenge, evaluate, and reinforce.

Every day brought a new challenge for which difficult decisions were made that impacted the psyches of teens. I welcomed this challenge. I wanted the responsibility to make a difference in each child. I didn't make excuses regarding socioeconomic status, family history, or academic disabilities. I chose the profession. Each day offered an opportunity to lead children to become learners. Beyond the classroom and playing field, I knew I could make an impact on their future. My colleagues and I teamed together to empower kids. I had a daily choice to make about my interactions with students. Because children are easily influenced, each spoken word has power.

Psychologist Dr. Haim Ginott (1972) captured the spirit of what teachers feel:

I've come to the frightening conclusion that I am the decisive element in the classroom. It's my daily mood that makes the weather. As a teacher, I possess a tremendous power to make a child's life miserable or joyous. I can be a tool of torture or an instrument of inspiration. I can humiliate or humor, hurt or heal. In all situations, it is my response that decides whether a crisis will be escalated or de-escalated and a child humanized or de-humanized. (p. 15)

Why would I want to exit the classroom to sit in an office marked "Principal?" Why leave behind chalk dust on my pants, riveting class discussions, teenage zits and zest, grading essays, and "ah ha" moments? I would be trading tranquility for turbulence. What was I thinking?

The answer is simple. Leading people on a larger scale was my destination. I was replaceable as a classroom teacher. There are others who shared my passion for teaching eighth-grade American history. Someone was always waiting in the wings to coach the sports teams. I believe I was intended to become a school administrator. Call it God's will—my manifest destiny. I knew it was time to become the head coach of a school instead of a classroom.

College classes on educational leadership cannot fully prepare someone for the complexity of the principalship. Practicums, internships, and other means of learning the craft do not provide the experiences one needs to lead multiple programs and people. Principals learn how to provide the necessary leadership for a school by trial and error, being mentored, reading, learning from mistakes, seeking feedback from others, and taking calculated risks. The job seems enormous at times. However, there are components of school leadership that when broken down into small parts, will provide a principal with the framework for creating a positive school environment.

Any success that I have had in school leadership is credited to what others formally or informally shared. My father was a leader as a church pastor. He modeled a relentless work ethic. An uncle empowered his staff. A college advisor instilled confidence. An assistant superintendent emphasized character. A university professor taught the art of teaching. A junior high coach demanded discipline. A human resource director modeled thoroughness in decision making. My mother and wife both exemplified the attribute of caring for others. A colleague reminded me about the importance of volunteerism and servitude. A former principal laughed and told stories. An assistant principal was resourceful and problem solved. These people and others in my life shaped my administrative career, and I am grateful.

A person I have never met has greatly influenced my leadership skills. This person is a successful college basketball coach. I am convinced that he is a better person than a coach based on the rapport that he develops with his family, staff, peers, and players. He does more than win basketball games: He leads young men to reach their potential. He molds them into a cohesive unit as they work toward a collective goal. He personally promotes and exhibits honesty, respect, passion, character, training, organization, purpose, and leadership. This is exactly what principals are trying to accomplish. In 24 years at Duke University, Mike Krzyzewski, a Hall of Fame coach and 12-time National Coach of the Year, has built a dynasty that few programs in the history of the game can match.

Krzyzewski's record as Duke's all-time winningest coach offers evidence of his leadership abilities. Even more impressive are the three national championships, including back-to-back titles in 1991 and 1992, that continue to make him the only coach since the University of California, Los Angeles's,

John Wooden with such an accomplishment. Coach K authored *Leading With the Heart: Successful Strategies for Basketball, Business and Life* (Krzyzewski, 2001). While reading the book, I found myself making countless applications about coaching a college basketball team and leading a school staff. The two parallel one another.

What are those critical components of educational leadership? I offer 10 tips on what school leaders, not just principals, can do to sustain a school setting that students and staff alike will appreciate and in which they will prosper. Plus, I believe that if the advice given is followed, a school leader will be rewarded in a variety of ways.

Tip 1—Hire People Who Are Willing to Be Part of a Team

A former colleague enjoyed hiring new teachers. He prided himself on keeping a stack of contracts in his top desk drawer that he pulled out to ask a prospective teacher to sign once the interview had concluded. He did not conduct a second interview. References were not checked. He did not ask the right questions to know if this teacher was going to be the right fit for the staff. He was not able to gauge whether the person had the capacity to learn new information, grow professionally, or support the goals of the organization. This poor approach haunted the school for years.

Selecting staff members may be the most important task of school administrators. Who you hire may end up being your legacy at the school. Effective hiring goes beyond selecting teachers: Savvy principals will employ secretaries, custodians, food service personnel, para-educators, and teacher aides who embrace the overall mission of the school.

Once on the school team, principals must ensure that new employees understand how important they are in educating children. Yes, every staff member—regardless of his or her job title—is part of the team that teaches kids. In fact, we all know of examples of the school custodian or secretary who serves as a role model for children. These support staff members can be the brightest part of a young person's day. Reinforce this theme throughout the school year in staff meetings, in new employee orientation sessions, and in writing.

All staff members should feel part of the team. Working independently does not offer the rewards of working collectively. People experience the power of a team concept when they work hard toward a common goal. They are in the trenches together. They conquer obstacles with one another. They overcome weaknesses by tapping the strengths of another teammate. They discover that their single contribution is a key ingredient in the overall recipe for success. Remember TEAM—Together Everyone Achieves More.

Tip 2—Your Staff and Students
Need Instant Belief in What You Say to Them

Addressing a staff for the very first time causes nervousness in even the strongest administrator. What should be said? What do people want to hear from their new leader? First impressions can last forever. The pressure is on to hit a home run. Another way to put it is: Whatever you do, don't strike out!

As corny as this may sound, practice aloud what you are going to say to your staff. Rehearse eye contact, pauses, and intonation. Would a basketball player forgo practicing free throws before the big game? Would a minister skip practicing a sermon before Sunday morning? Absolutely not. It is imperative that employees and children experience your credibility from the start. Kids are particularly keen in seeing through adults. People expect substance, not style. Deliver your beliefs with conviction. Staff members want to be led and to intrinsically know their leader is believable from the very beginning.

Tip 3—Leaders Instill Respect by Having a Caring Attitude

If you can accomplish Tip 3 on a regular basis, you can take your school to great heights. I really believe this. The great part of this advice is that it is pretty simple to accomplish. Once achieved, staff members will be able to forgive your poor decisions, sense your compassion for others, and understand that a principal has to make difficult decisions. Caring means showing a genuine interest in people's well-being and who they are. Examples of a principal's caring include doing the following:

- Learn the names of staff members' children.
- Invite spouses to visit the school.
- Notice something special in a classroom.
- Inquire about an event in people's lives (birthday, anniversary, death).
- Go the extra mile to assist a staff member in need of something.
- Organize a group of kids to sweep snow off staff members' vehicles so they will not have to.
- Compliment an act of kindness.
- Leave a voice mail or note for a staff member that simply says, "Thank you for being a positive influence at our school."
- Send a bouquet of flowers to a person you just hired.
- Cover a class period for a colleague so he or she can take an extended lunch with a friend or relative.
- Provide personal or professional counseling.

- Provide snacks or meals on professional development days.
- Convey to people that hearing what they have to share with you is the most important thing that you have to do right now (even when it isn't).
- Meet deadlines and obligations.

It has been said that people don't care what you know; they just want to know that you care. When staff members know that you care about them and for them, they will respect your authority. They will support you even when it is difficult. They will implement new programs. Teach differently. Promote the positive. Accept constructive criticism. Focus on what is right. Better yet, teachers and students will initiate caring behaviors if modeled by their principal. You will notice that your school environment is thriving. The climate is conducive for acceptance, concern, and compassion for others. Staff and students flourish. Once this is established, it will transcend toward parents, community members, and other stakeholders in your school.

To keep a caring concept on the front burner of our school program, teachers are given a visual reminder. Distributed to each teacher is a business card on which the word CARE is written on the left side with the following message:

Compliment as many people as you can every day.

Act in your teammates' best interests.

Respect the differences in others.

Extend a helping hand.

Tip 4—Meet the Truth Head-On

A principal makes a myriad of daily decisions. Some decisions are not easily made. The situation requires understanding the complexity of the matter, careful deliberation, and effective resolution. There are situations a principal cannot ignore. Examples include the following:

- Teacher is using inappropriate language around children.
- Staff member is using the Internet to surf pornographic Web sites.
- Parent is harassing a teacher.
- Secretary is not friendly to visitors.
- Bus driver touches a student in anger.
- Concession stand operator is pocketing profits.

- Coach's demands on players are unwarranted.
- Assistant principal fails to support you publicly.
- School nurse errs in dispensing medication.
- Counselor did not report child abuse to the appropriate authorities.

Effective principals do not sweep problems under the carpet. They don't discount them, hoping that they go away. Does a coach fail to address a player who is detrimental to the team? Does the plant manager close his eyes on the employee who is preventing productivity? If one ignores the physical symptoms of an ailing body, the body begins to fail. Medical advice is sought. A doctor prescribes medication. People will not get better unless the problem is brought to their attention. The best medicine for an ailing staff member is a dose of the principal.

Administrators regularly work with thorny situations. Decisions are made that have a lasting impact on people. Difficult solutions to complicated matters are life changing. My experience tells me that people want to be held accountable. Internally, they are struggling with the decisions that they have made. They experience angst. Mentally and physically, they may not be sound. Guilt is prevalent.

People make choices that are not congruent with your belief system. Confront these situations head-on. Collect facts. Listen. Care. Discover the truth. Seek input regarding resolution. Document. Expect change. Monitor. Express hope.

I know what you are thinking: There are times when a problem does not go away despite your best efforts. What do you do? My advice may involve more than one of the following, depending on the situation:

- Take small steps toward the intended outcome. Reinforce the positives along the way.
- Try a new approach in solving the problem.
- Involve others to assist in the desired change.
- Be patient. Change doesn't happen suddenly.
- There is strength in numbers. Attain support from your boss.
- Realize what works for one person may not be the best for another.
- Reprimand, suspend, or dismiss an employee if necessary.

Gain credibility with students, teachers, support staff, peers, and central office administrators by your willingness to confront the truth without hesitation. Avoidance leads to destruction. Harm occurs. Children's lives are adversely affected. School climate disintegrates. Complacency sets in. There are no easy ways out. Effective administrators know this, but more important, confront it. It takes courage to make tough decisions; don't chicken out. Reverend Martin Luther King Jr. keenly defined courage when he said, "The ultimate measure of a man is not where he stands in moments of comfort and convenience, but where he stands at a time of challenge and controversy" (see http://www.lmiuru.com/quotes.html).

Tip 5—Students, Staff, and Parents Expect You to Be Upbeat, Positive, and Confident All the Time

The first four tips have all dealt with working and communicating with people. So does this one, because this is a people business. If you are contemplating entering the school leadership circle and do not have a naturally high comfort level working with people, pursue other avenues. As an educational leader in your building, you are constantly under the microscope. People instinctively judge their boss. Privately, they will bring attention to the car you drive, the clothes you wear, the voice in which you speak, and how you carry yourself. They judge your verbal and nonverbal communication. Your demeanor in all settings is critiqued—at the grocery store, at church, at ball games, in meetings, in hallways, in the cafeteria, and in the neighborhood. You will be a discussion topic from the faculty lounge to the post office.

I felt this expectation (and even pressure) when I was teaching too. Kids want their teacher to be dynamic every day. They want to see smiles, enthusiasm, and self-assurance. These attributes are contagious. When modeled by any educator, a positive learning atmosphere is created. Leadership expert John C. Maxwell (2003) noted that a positive attitude is absolutely essential if people desire to be effective leaders. In fact, attitude not only determines one's level of contentment as a person, but it also impacts how others will interact with you.

Charisma is the word that captures what I am trying to say. World leaders, star athletes, celebrities, and corporate executives often have magnetic personalities. Charisma includes charm, warmth, excitement, and self-assurance. Charisma does not include being cocky, boastful, flamboyant, or pompous. I believe charisma is instinctual. Some folks just seem to be born with it. However, there are examples of what principals can do to enhance how they are viewed by others. Remember—image is important to your success. Consider the following:

- Dress professionally each day.
- Groom yourself to appear neat and clean.

- Smile frequently.
- Greet others with enthusiasm and genuine interest.
- Keep your head up—glow facially.
- Walk with a sense of purpose.
- Shake hands in a manner that demonstrates strength.
- Initiate verbal contact with others in social settings.
- Seek out others when you are on or off duty—in the lunchroom, at ball games, at parent/teacher conferences, in the parking lot, at community events, and standing in line.
- Counter negative statements with positive remarks.
- Exchange "we can" beliefs when responding to negative people.
- Fill yourself with a diet of healthy thinking.
- Condition your mind to never experience pessimism.
- Maximize your strengths to overshadow your weaknesses.
- Maintain your mental and physical health.

My advice to all administrators entering the profession is to always be yourself. If the items listed do not fit to who you are, don't attempt them foolishly. However, look at this list again. I cannot imagine that any of these would be risky or unadvisable. If they become a natural part of who you are, which may take some practice, you will influence others. People will want to be around you. You can articulate the mission of the school. Your vision for student success can be expressed. You will inspire. You will motivate. You will spark change. You will make a difference as the leader of your school.

Tip 6—Create a Circle So People Do Not Feel Like They Are in a Corner

Coach Krzyzewski (2001) used the analogy of an infant plant to explain the importance of allowing people to maximize their abilities. He pointed out that if you put a plant in a jar, its growth is limited by the shape of the jar. But if you allow it to grow freely, there is no limit to the size the plant may grow. Coach K then reminded us that there are four freedoms that should be assured by every leader in every organization: the freedom to grow personally, to make mistakes and learn from them, to work hard, and to be yourself. What application does Coach K's analogy have for school administrators? His advice included specific suggestions that are applicable for school leaders:

- Hire people who bring something fresh to your team of teachers.
- Hire teachers who are not clones of yourself or others.
- Choose people who thirst for knowledge and want new experiences each day.
- Automatically go into a mode of listening and acceptance when you are approached with new ideas. Do not robotically put up barriers.
- Ask your team members to attend seminars, mentor a colleague, participate in educational research, take college courses, and present at conferences.
- Share your knowledge and expertise with others. Remember, the plant needs nourishment and sunshine, and you may be its provider.
- Understand that people are going to make mistakes. In fact, mistakes can be advantageous because we learn what doesn't work.
- Mistakes are made, but do not punish unless absolutely necessary.
- Encourage risk taking and thinking outside of the box.
- Don't have too many rules in your building. Rules stifle creativity.
- Foster an environment that encourages sharing opinions and trying new things.
- Accept different teaching styles and educational approaches.
- Do not give up on reluctant staff members. Old dogs can learn new tricks.
- Show willingness on your part to grow freely. When others notice the principal showing innovativeness, they will spark a chain reaction.
- Be alert that creativity can come from unexpected personnel.

I spoke with our head custodian in the cafeteria one morning. Several students were eating breakfast before school. The bell rang for the kids to go to their first-hour class. Some students arrived after the bell rang and wanted to eat breakfast. They explained their bus usually runs later than the other buses. They felt like they should still be able to eat breakfast. In fact, a couple of the kids qualified for free or reduced-price breakfasts, and it was important they should have a good meal. I had no way of knowing if the students told me the truth about their bus arriving later on a regular basis. I did not want them taking advantage of the situation. I preferred that they arrive at the first hour on time. I struggled with how to handle the matter.

The custodian heard my plight. In a nonchalant manner, he said, "Why don't you create a bus pass that the driver gives to the child who arrives late to school?" He continued by saying that adults should control the situation, not the kids. Students show their pass to the kitchen workers, eat their breakfast, and then go to their first hour. The student gives the laminated bus pass to the teacher who accepts their excused tardy. The bus pass is recycled back to the bus company so that it can be used again.

Guess what? This idea worked beautifully. The custodian offered a simple solution for what I had made into a complex problem. The end result made everyone a winner; the students' problem had been addressed, the custodian felt pride and had been reaffirmed that he worked in an environment in which he could make suggestions, and the principal had a workable solution to a sticky problem.

Do not force staff and students into a corner. If you want people to think outside the box, create a circle! Bottom line—let others share their solutions, talents, and creativity for the betterment of the school.

Tip 7—Ask Stakeholders Their Opinion

Have you had your boss ask you for your opinion? Everyone feels an internal sensation of importance when their opinion really means something. We like to know when our input is valued. Endorphins are released. Typically, an enthusiastic and thoughtful response is given. Even if your boss doesn't take your advice or follow up the way you think he or she should, it still feels good to share your opinion.

Seek opinions from a wide variety of stakeholders. This includes board of education members, community leaders, parents, peers, teachers, noncertified staff, assistant principals, retired administrators, family members, local ministers, business representatives, and most of all, students. If you want to break down barriers with an adversary, seek out his or her point of view.

Leaders are tempted to make decisions without viewing the outlook of others. School administrators tend to rely on sound judgment and experience. Gathering the viewpoints of others takes time. School principals do not have excess time on their hands. Sometimes it is just easier to move forward without soliciting a lot of input. Don't sacrifice the golden opportunity to survey others just to save time.

Consider the positive consequences of asking stakeholders their opinions:

- A team concept is promoted.
- Opinions can present differing sides to an issue that had not been considered.
- Facts emerge.

- Well-rounded judgments are formed.
- Dissenting points of view are respected.
- People experience influence when they have been involved in decision making.
- Complaints are less likely to occur.
- Enthusiasm is generated.
- People feel empowered.
- The principal receives support.

Remember that trust is a key component when discussing opinions. Stakeholders must know that their opinions are safe to be shared and negative repercussions will not ensue. Gratitude is expressed by the person seeking opinions. A wise principal will publicly credit others for contributing to the final decision that is made.

Tip 8—Faith, Family, and Friends Prioritize Decision Making

Educators can be easily stressed. The demands on time and commitment increase daily, particularly with the NCLB mandate. With outside school responsibilities, school personnel have additional pressures. It is very important that all staff members understand that school is not their highest priority. Surprisingly, at our school, it ranks pretty low.

As schools dedicate their efforts to raising test scores, data are used in driving the decisions on how to best accomplish this task. Getting accurate information is helpful when making vital decisions. As a principal, I use Tip 8 frequently when responding to the requests of staff members and parents. I collect data from the three Fs: If their need involves faith, family, or friend issues, typically the request is kindly accepted and granted. For example, a parent shares that his or her family had a church activity that evening that prevented him or her from attending Back to School Night. This helps me understand the parent's absence from this important school event. If a teacher asks to arrive at school late to see a friend before the friend goes into surgery, support will be given. A secretary is called into the principal's office to discuss an uncharacteristic negative demeanor toward others. The secretary explains that his or her child is disrupting the home environment, which has caused great stress. This helps me understand that this family issue needs greater attention. I may try to rearrange job responsibilities during this difficult time. Time off may be given to meet with a family counselor. My demonstration of caring in itself will also assist in improving the situation.

Our jobs are not the most important part of our lives. Staff members are told if they are to be solid employees, their faith, family, and friends must come first. To drive home this message, I use a stool as an example. If one leg of a stool is weak, the stool will collapse. The other two legs will not be able to support the weight. The stool will not be able to function properly.

The same is true for human beings. If our faith, family, and friends are not stable, we will falter. We must continually nurture these three areas in our life. If they are strong, like a three-legged stool, school personnel will be able to perform their jobs much better.

Emphasis is also placed on the flipside of this principle. Not only should we nurture the three Fs, we must allow our faith, family, and friends to reciprocate the deed. This is difficult for educators. Teachers, counselors, and administrators tend to be givers, not receivers. Principals must counsel staff to accept help from others when they need it. Humility and pride sometimes have to be set aside when receiving a helping hand.

Tip 9—Establish Tradition

My wife is big on tradition. During the holiday season, our family faithfully repeats the same rituals year after year. Our three children understand that when it is Christmas time, Mom will insist on fulfilling our traditions (i.e, cutting down the tree, eating breakfast casserole after presents are opened, giving Dad one silly gift in honor of a deceased grandparent). Despite our gentle criticisms of Mom's holiday customs, we all understand their importance. Repeating something together can be meaningful. It is like the cheerleading squad that constantly shouts out a chant—it becomes stronger and stronger as it is repeated over and over. Duplication brings strength. A commonality is shared that brings people together.

In school settings, most people use the word *tradition* in reference to a sports team. A team with strong tradition possesses a winning edge. Perennial powerhouse football teams masterfully promote their traditions. Successful coaches speak about tradition at every opportunity. As a principal, if you want to create something special in your building, instill tradition!

Tradition is alive and well at Wheatridge Middle School. We have established these traditions in a short amount of time. Some examples include the following:

- Before the first day of school, we have a family potluck dinner for all staff.
- At the dinner, employees introduce their family members.

- After the dinner, we gather all the children for a photograph. An enlarged copy of the photo is framed and placed in the staff lounge. The pictures of the children are never taken down.
- Former teachers and administrators are invited to special events. This allows our school history to be kept alive.
- An old school bell is rung after a football touchdown.
- If teachers are given permission to leave before their duty day is over, I announce on the public address system that there is a tie sale at the main gate. It sounds silly, but it is a long-standing tradition.
- We give out the Golden Apple Award every six weeks to teachers who have made outstanding contributions to the school. The trophy is given from colleague to colleague.
- In January, all staff members are invited to a nice dinner for fellowship, gag gifts, and relaxation.
- In May, staff members and their families are invited to attend a professional baseball game. Prizes are given throughout the evening.
- Every year, we take a picture of our staff. The photo is placed in the front lobby in a display area with pictures from previous years.
- Community service and charitable acts are trademarks for our students and staff.

Tradition inspires people. It makes them want more. They want to come back. They want the journey to continue. Tradition feels good. It fosters strength and unity. It is difficult to destroy or criticize. Tradition can be an ally for a principal.

Tip 10—Thank Everyone for the Journey

When I was a child, just before I would walk out the door to go to a birthday party or to someone's house for lunch or dinner, my parents would always remind me to say thank you. Expressing thanks to anyone who does something for you was the expectation from Mom and Dad. Principals, too, need to heed this great advice.

As leaders of many, principals have ample opportunity to express appreciation to others. Be intentional about this. Giving thanks should be a habit. Committee members, parent/teacher association representatives, secretaries, board of education members, student council members, custodians, bus drivers, coaches, and sponsors are just a few examples of people deserving your gratitude. These groups work hard to put the school in a positive light. Be specific about what you are thankful for. Go the extra mile and accompany your appreciation with a gift or surprise.

The journey sometimes feels like a marathon. The school year races along with obstacles along the way. We tire but always find that little extra energy to cross the finish line. The close of the school year marks the end of the educational expedition. You can take the opportunity to compliment everyone for their efforts in making the journey successful. Always say thank you!

You just finished Tim's top 10 tips for leadership. Hopefully, you will be inspired to be an exemplary leader in your school building. There are many aspects to being a leader in addition to the 10 critical components that were discussed here. Enhance your leadership capabilities by working with a mentor, stay abreast of leadership research, and sharpen your individual skills. Twenty-first-century schools are clamoring for outstanding leaders. Congratulations on empowering your students, staff, parents, and community.

Two Essential Leadership Qualities

Mark Roherty
Mequon, Wisconsin

Over the last 15 years as a high school principal and the 9 years prior to that as an assistant principal, I often have been asked my view as to the most important qualities that a leader needs to exhibit. Many esteemed authors of books and articles have researched and defined leadership in understandable and meaningful ways, but in my estimation from the baseline of personal experience, the best practice of leadership is reflected through showing appreciation and visibility.

A principal, first of all, has the privilege of being in charge of a wide spectrum of adults, including classroom teachers, secretaries, custodians, hall supervisors, paraprofessionals, nurses, parent volunteers, coaches, advisors, and other significant contributors to the mission of educating children. Each person provides a talent or gift that never should be overlooked, for acknowledgments of the good things that are being done on behalf of children are powerful forces in creating a school culture in which people work together and students and adults achieve success. There should be no hesitation on the part of a leader to express appreciation, because in effect, he or she is shaping a school atmosphere built on trust and a sense of community.

A second quality at the core of successful leadership is visibility. This means that a principal needs to be available and present to students, staff, and parents. Sensible time management allows an open-door policy and excursions up and down the hallways and into the classrooms, the cafeteria, the gym, and the receiving room throughout the day. It also means being a member of committees; attending multiple meetings; hosting parent coffees; showing up at school club activities, athletic events, musical and drama performances; and so forth. That kind of commitment often implies five minutes for a quick sandwich at lunch, a shortened supper hour, and multiple evenings at school every week, but there is personal satisfaction in believing that you have made a positive difference at the end of each day.

Leaders need to reflect on the powerful impact that showing appreciation and being visible can have on the school community. The growing complexity and challenge of a principal's job can be handled more effectively when these qualities are internalized.

GOOD LEADERS ASK GOOD QUESTIONS

Tommy Floyd
Somerset, Kentucky

Although it is one of the most demanding positions in public education, the principalship is the necessary leadership driving force behind school improvement. In fact, true school improvement cannot occur without the principal, because this is the place where the rubber hits the road every day for kids. But the wonderful thing about the principalship is that this is a place where you can make a real difference for kids! To be the best principals that we can be, we should ask ourselves the following questions:

- What was my teaching experience like?
- How well do I understand the requirements for good instruction?
- How well can I recognize barriers to success?
- Why do I want to be an administrator?
- What does it take to act as a positive or negative force day to day?
- How well do I resist the urge to personalize any and every negative? There will be many.
- How well do I delegate responsibility? I cannot do it all.
- What are my long-term professional goals? How long can I stand the heat?
- How focused can I remain on instructional issues amid the never-ending barrier parade? I will be required to change channels every few minutes.
- How well do I stay focused on the big picture? Here comes the minutia!
- What leadership experiences do I bring versus management experiences?
- There is a big difference between management and leadership! Do I know the difference?
- How well can I maintain composure with a pace that never slows and requires good decision making? Every decision is important, and most can bite you.
- Can I find satisfaction by being behind the scenes?

You do not even want to think about becoming a principal if seeing all students find success is not one of your most positive goals. When you have wrapped your mind around all of these questions and know where you stand, you are ready to embrace the principalship. Remember, always keep in mind the "big five":

1. Don't panic.

2. Don't get in a hurry.

3. Don't give out too much information.

4. Don't get mad.

5. Put kids first every time.

LEADERSHIP BEST PRACTICES: IN RETROSPECT

Kristine Servais
DeKalb, Illinois

Best practices reflect a desire to create and demonstrate excellence. I began my first principalship with only six months of leadership experience as an assistant principal and while still in the process of finishing my formal training. Yet my first instinct was to provide students with best practices in teaching and learning. Bay View Middle School was in the process of growing in size and transitioning from a junior high to a middle school. I was a rookie as a principal, but fortunately, I brought with me a great deal of successful middle school experience from my role as a teacher. So the first question was: Where do I start?

Beginning Goals

I began my principalship with three goals. My first goal was to provide a safe and vitalized learning environment for students and staff. This would require establishing best practices in the middle school while also developing an identity unique to our teachers and students. Second, great tasks require teamwork, and I would strive to place teaming as a centerpiece to accomplishing all of our work. My third goal was to provide leadership that would empower students and teachers to function as a successful learning community.

Leadership Beliefs: An Internal Compass

My goals as a beginning principal called for leadership strategies in modeling, collaboration, and student-centered decision making. It would take three to five years to systematically accomplish these goals. From the very beginning, I saw the potential in this staff and community to be a high-performing school. My beliefs were fundamental in my role and responsibility as a leader. In an exercise conducted by my superintendent during my first year as a principal, all the district administrators were required to identify their primary beliefs. These became my guide, my compass for decision making. These first beliefs were

- A safe and caring environment is the foundation of learning for children and adults.

- An educational leader's greatest responsibility is to provide every child with caring and competent teachers.
- Learning is a daily and lifelong process whereby leadership lessons can be learned from risk taking, adversity, and failure.

Today I still carry these with me as a reminder of the internal compass each of us as leaders must have in making decisions that impact students and teachers.

Cultural Change

One of my primary beliefs is that a safe and caring environment is essential for students and teachers to be successful. Bay View was rapidly growing, and although order and safety were adequate in the classroom, they were not provided in areas such as the hallways, cafeteria, and playground. Teachers agreed that greater safety was needed, but there was not a commitment or unified responsibility to provide a healthier environment for students outside of each teacher's classroom. Middle school students were not entering Bay View each day assured of emotional, physical, and social safety. My top priority was to determine ways in which we could provide a safe and successful learning community for our students. This would begin by placing students at the center of all our decisions, beginning with an emphasis on schoolwide safety and responsible student behavior. This would be the first of many cultural changes that would take place.

Students First

One of my first strategies was to model student-centered leadership. The premise of every decision I made was "How is this good for kids?" One way to convince teachers of how students must be placed at the heart of all decisions was to visit other successful middle schools. We spent time in other schools observing best middle school practices and talked with teachers who reinforced the belief that students come first. To see it was to believe it. Next, we began to explore ways we could make schoolwide changes to better meet the social, physical, and emotional developmental needs of adolescents. This would require the development of a middle school identity, and to get there would require teamwork. We developed a taskforce to create and implement a schoolwide approach to recognize responsible and safe behavior. Even though this was difficult at first, over time, we accepted it as the curriculum of any responsive middle school to adolescent development.

Project STRIDE

The results were remarkable. A schoolwide program called Project STRIDE was designed and implemented. It was the result of long hours of collegial conversations among teachers on creating and recognizing successful student performance. This performance was described as the A, B, Cs of the program: academics, behavior, and citizenship. STRIDE was an acronym that represented the emerging ideals of the Bay View school community: Students Taking Responsibility for Demonstrating Excellence. The identity of the school and Project STRIDE was symbolically represented by a high-top tennis shoe. We placed this symbol throughout the school, in the handbook, on T-shirts, and on banners. Students were active participants in implementing a program that honored success in academics, responsible school behavior, and service to their school and community. The identity of Bay View changed as a result of Project STRIDE. Bay View literally became one of the schools we had visited a few years earlier.

Time for Teaming

Everything I knew as an educator and leader told me that teaming would be critical to our success. Following the work of Peter Senge (1990), I knew that teams, not individuals, would be the basic learning unit in our organization. As he said, unless the team can learn, the organization cannot. The development of teams became important both as a process and a product for Bay View as a learning community. First, this would require my commitment and ability to redesign the master schedule to include common planning time for teams. I began with the goal to not only create team time for grade-level teachers, but to also include every applied arts teacher, counselor, and special-education teacher on a team. We would increase the likelihood of meeting the diverse needs of our students if we could develop highly effective teams. To do this, we would need to identify and implement best practices in teaming.

Failure Is Just Not an Option

We began with a new master schedule that created opportunities for teaming to improve student achievement and success. Daily team time allowed teachers to develop a team identity, guiding principles, goals, and handbooks reflective of themselves and their students. For example, the Apollo Team was made up of a flight crew of teachers and parents, had a flight manual as a handbook, and had the motto "Failure is not an option." Staff development and resources such as the National Middle School Association, Katzenbach and Smith's (2003) *The Wisdom of Teams,* John Maxwell's (2003) *The 17 Indisputable Laws of Teamwork,* and middle school experts such as Chris Stevenson contributed to our team development. Once teams were developed, we were able to provide a school-within-a-school approach. Grade-level teams were composed of three to five teachers and 75 students in what we called houses. Students could experience a greater sense of safety, belonging, and personal commitment to successful learning in each house under the direction of an effective teaching team. Team development was pivotal and became the turning point for Bay View as a successful learning community.

CARE for Students

There is an expression that became a motto for me as a principal: People don't care how much you know, until they know how much you care. One of the groups for which our school needed to provide greater educational services was our at-risk students. We began to examine ways we could provide extra assistance for students who demonstrated at-risk behaviors. The program was called CARE: Children at Risk in Education. Ten students per grade were identified and provided with a class offered by a qualified guidance counselor. This class recognized school, social, and individual conditions in students' lives that made them at risk of not graduating from high school. The CARE program was another step for Bay View to serve students of different needs through the best instruction and learning conditions possible.

Increasing Leadership Capacity

There is no one size fits all in a successful middle school. Adolescents by their very nature come in all shapes and sizes. As a principal, I discovered that teachers, too, range dramatically in their skills, needs, and performances. This required me to develop my transformational leadership skills to build relationships as well as programs suited to the needs of adults and students. My third goal was to provide leadership that would empower students and teachers to function as a successful learning community. I realized to transform the culture to a successful middle school, we would need to increase leadership capacity among students, parents, and teachers.

Visible Presence

My commitment to be visibly present with students, parents, and teachers, and a philosophy of people over paper, demanded long hours. Consequently, it meant that paperwork went home with me each evening and every weekend. As leaders, we must leave our office and be visibly present in our organizations to build relationships. I began to use school walk-throughs as a means to visit more classrooms and better get to know my teachers. Steven Covey (1989) suggested that leaders must be effective in time management by demonstrating "first things first." As a principal, I tried to prioritize my time for students, parents, and staff. The demands of leadership were high, but so were the results. Bay View was selected as a National Blue Ribbon School in 1994. First, we celebrated. Then we came to the realization that our success as a middle school was only the tip of the iceberg in terms of where we could go next.

Student Empowerment

While we were being considered as a National Blue Ribbon School, the evaluator shared with me some of the student comments that he had heard during his visit. Students had explained to him how students governed the school. They explained that through the middle school advisory program, a student representative was selected from each of 50 groups, and these student representatives served as a council for all school decisions. There was little or no mention of me as the principal. I realized that my efforts for student empowerment had succeeded.

It is difficult as a principal to determine a clear image of who one is to others. One of my favorite descriptions was entered in a writing contest by a seventh grader named Stephanie. She described me in the following essay:

A strong, passionate principal can change a school from a good school to an excellent school. The principal can be the key to an enthusiastic staff and willing students. A principal can encourage teachers to start great programs and projects that get the students involved. She can challenge the staff and students by having high expectations and addressing the important school rules. A strong principal isn't afraid to take risks and get the middle school involved in the community and other impressive projects. A passionate principal will make the staff want to work hard to please her, so they are more likely to be more creative and energetic toward the students. This will make the students more involved. On the other hand, if a principal stays hidden and isn't very involved in the school, the staff will not be very motivated by her expectations. It will have a negative effect on the student body as well. A principal has the most influence over the entire school.

Leadership Fitness

Leadership is hard work. Those of us called to leadership may even claim it was not a choice. For me, everything I do is a choice. As a leader, I made choices in the best interests of students. (Teachers told me after I left Bay View that each of them knew that before they could approach me on any issue or request, they would have to respond to my question: How is this good for kids?) Leaders also make important choices to balance their lives physically, emotionally, mentally, and spiritually. Steven Covey's (1989) *7 Habits* calls for sharpening the saw. When we fail to take care of ourselves as leaders, we become less effective and less productive. It was important for me during my principalship to find time to exercise, to reflect, and to remain spiritually strong.

One way in which leaders can remain healthy and productive is through the support of a mentor. Leaders need to find mentors who will support and lift them up when the load of leadership becomes too heavy. Parker Palmer (1998), in *The Courage to Teach,* emphasized that the human soul requires time, conversation, and trust. Time, a most precious commodity to the busy school leader, is a gift we give to one another to develop and sustain a mentoring relationship. This gift benefits both partners in a mentoring relationship. The choice to mentor increases leadership capacity for ourselves and those around us. I have only had three mentors in my career as a leader. Each one was vital to provide feedback, criticism, and support when needed. I consider mentoring a lifeline for sustaining healthy leadership.

Celebrating Together

Finally, leaders must learn to celebrate the many successes as a school community. Celebrating is a form of nourishment for leaders and those they serve. Celebrations allow us to recognize the values and performances of individuals, teams, and our learning culture. Celebrations should not be limited to big events such as being selected as a national high-performing school. A favorite resource, *Encouraging the Heart* (Kouzes & Posner, 1998), helped me to realize that to sustain top performance, people need encouragement. The authors are leading authorities in leadership development and suggest that we encourage others when we set clear standards, expect the best, pay attention to people, set the example, and celebrate together. Public celebration at Bay View was a gradual cultural change in which recognition was not limited to students, but also grew into traditions in which teacher accomplishments were acknowledged.

Many of my celebrations as a transformational leader occurred through building relationships and empowering those who matter most in our school—the students. Faculty meetings, quarterly grading periods, and end-of-the-year events at Bay View became a time to celebrate. Project STRIDE included quarterly celebrations for success in academics, responsible behavior, and citizenship. Celebrations are not the sole responsibility of the leader. It became everyone's responsibility in the Bay View community to recognize success, and this recognition took the form of cards, awards, thank-yous, and personal recognition. Teams developed rituals within their houses in which celebrations and honoring adolescent development and success became a part of our middle school curriculum.

One of my favorite celebrations as a principal occurred each year on the final day of school. As the final dismissal bell rang, I would play the "Hallelujah Chorus" over the loud speaker for the entire school of 900 students, all the teachers, and many visiting parents. Even the superintendent and district office staff located in our building would leave their offices to join in the fun. It resulted in a chorus of schoolwide laughter and a reminder to me of the continued need to celebrate our work and ourselves as leaders.

My Leadership Journey

I left my principalship at Bay View in the spring of 1998. We had literally and educationally grown from a traditional junior high school in 1989 to a high-performing and nationally recognized middle school by 1998. Today, Richard DuFour and Robert Eaker (1998) would describe Bay View's development as a professional learning community consisting of best practices for enhancing student achievement. I realize there is no one best practice or any single leadership effort that fosters the growth and success of a learning community. Today I am a professor of educational leadership. I encourage future principals to courageously follow their passion to make a difference in the lives of children. School leaders choose a road less traveled, and it can be an amazing journey. As I continue in this journey, I hope to provide a path for the next generation of principals who also choose to travel this road.

If you are considering becoming a principal, truly understand the brave new world of education that you will be attempting to lead. We are seeing increasing student populations, rising diversity, decreases in school budgets, and an alarming teacher shortage at the same time we will be facing an unprecedented area of accountability, highlighted by NCLB. Although the challenge for principals will be greater than ever, the need for excellent people to aspire to this position has never been more vital.

SNAPSHOTS

Sharing a Vision

Brent Curtice
Paonia, Colorado

Having a staff that shares my vision for student success has enabled our school community to strive for the excellence that is our goal. As a goal-oriented person, I have always had a direction and a vision for Paonia High School; however, through my meeting with a group of highly motivated staff members on a weekly basis, a clearly articulated plan for student achievement based on solid research has evolved.

As a leader, I not only have encouraged staff participation in developing our goals, but I have also provided departments with time to align seventh- to twelfth-grade curricula with what we want to accomplish to ensure greater student success and achievement. Knowing that staff acceptance is vital to the success of any program, I have spent the time to articulate and explain my vision to the staff, who have bought into my vision that the ACT is a proven measure of student progress; hence, our curriculum is ACT driven. We use the data from the ACT to track student progress and to identify areas that need remediation. I also encourage pedagogical innovation and the sophisticated use of technology to help us achieve our goals and to provide students with as many options as possible.

Empower Others

Kevin Fillgrove
Ephrata, Pennsylvania

Often, administrators feel they must be able to do everything, and do it well—no one can do that. So, find something you are good at that will overshadow your weaknesses. Then, surround yourself with others who will fill in those weaknesses. Find people's strengths and exploit them. Identify people who are strong, and surround yourself with them. I have found that if you spend most of your time with the best teachers, your school will excel.

Balancing Life as a Leader

Lyman Goding
Plymouth, Massachusetts

Hmm . . . balanced personal life for a principal. . . . I don't think I ever got this exactly right, but here are a couple of thoughts:

1. Join the state principal association or regional groups. Our jobs are so lonely at times, but I found a real family through our state group (the Massachusetts Secondary School Administrators Association). Whether it is the Association of Supervision and Curriculum Development, National Association of Secondary School Principals, National Association of Elementary School Principals, or another group, a place to share, consult, and create a critical friends support group has been refreshing and inspirational.

2. For my family, which I often ignore for weeks at a time—including weekends—I found that sharing the calendar in the same way I would with my secretary and other staff was helpful at home as well.

3. Block out time for family: We bought several club or timeshare weeks in the summer to force me to spend family time since it was already paid for and committed!

4. Find others to do your work for you . . . my secretary is much smarter than I am at so many things—especially when she knows what I need . . . my assistants appreciate being given responsibilities beyond discipline and do them very well. Figure out what you do well and what is most important, and accept that other things might not

get the same attention. Example: My passion is the art and science of teaching and learning strategy and being the "principal teacher."

... And Don't Forget

Heath Morrison
Waldorf, Maryland

Ensure that all of your decisions are based on the framework and philosophy of doing what is best for students and instruction. School stakeholders may disagree with your choices, but they will not disagree with the reasons for your decisions.

Summary

Leadership Research: Set direction, develop people, redesign the organization, understand how to support teachers, manage the curriculum, promote student learning, enable powerful teaching to occur, and support student learning.

Best Practice Ideas for Leadership
From Award-Winning Secondary School Principals

- Work toward shared goals
- Communicate the vision
- Be purposeful
- Be reflective
- Design and redesign the organization
- Promote student learning
- Be visible
- Empower staff and students
- Provide ongoing training for staff
- Do not accept failure
- Do what is best for kids
- Say thank you

LEADERSHIP REFLECTION

1. Where is my leadership strong?

2. What are leadership needs at my school?

3. Am I cultivating leadership at every level of the school?

4. In what ways am I doing this?

5. Does the school community have a shared vision for our school?

6. What am I doing now to promote our shared vision?

7. What am I doing to support people?

8. What am I doing to actively design and redesign our organization?

9. What ideas in this chapter will be helpful to strengthen leadership at our school?

10. How can we implement these ideas in our school?

11. How might these ideas need to be revised to be successful at our school?

ADDITIONAL RESOURCES

ACT
http://www.act.org/aap

Dupont Leadership Training
http://www.dupont.com/corp/social/people

KASAB—Linda Munger and Joellen Killion
http://www.aea9.k12.ia.us/download/00/communicatorpdfs/
09_10_2004.pdf

Mike Krzyzewski
http://www.coachk.com

Lightspan
http://www.studyweb.com

John Maxwell
http://www.leadershipnow.com/leadershop/johnmaxwell.html

National Staff Development Council
http://www.nsdc.org

New Jersey Writing Project
http://www.njwpt.com

SchoolNet
http://www.schoolnet.com

REFERENCES

Covey, S. (1989). *The 7 habits of highly effective people: Powerful lessons in personal change.* New York: Simon & Schuster.

Davies, B. (Ed.). (2005). *The essentials of school leadership.* Thousand Oaks, CA: Corwin Press.

Davis, S., Darling-Hammond, L., LaPointe, M., & Meyerson, D. (2005). *School leadership study: Developing successful principals.* Stanford, CA: Stanford Educational Leadership Institute.

DuFour, R., & Eaker, R. (1998). *Professional learning communities at work: Best practices for enhancing student achievement.* Bloomington, IN: National Educational Service.

Garmston, R., & Wellman, B. (1999). *The adaptive school: A sourcebook for developing collaborative groups.* Norwood, MA: Christopher-Gordon.

Ginott, H. (1972). *Between teacher and child.* New York: Macmillan.

Hallinger, P., & Heck, R. (1999). Next generation methods for the study of leadership and school improvement. In J. Murphy & K. S. Lewis (Eds.), *Handbook of research on educational administration* (2nd ed., pp. 141–162). San Francisco: Jossey-Bass.

Katzenbach, J. R., & Smith, D. K. (2003). *The wisdom of teams.* New York: Harper-Collins.

Kouzes, J. M., & Posner, B. Z. (1998). *Encouraging the heart.* San Francisco: Jossey-Bass.

Krzyzewski, M. (2001). *Leading with the heart: Successful strategies for basketball, business, and life.* New York: Warner Books.

Leithwood, K., & Jantzi, D. (2005). Transformational leadership. In B. Davies (Ed.), *The essentials of school leadership* (pp. 31–43). Thousand Oaks, CA: Corwin Press.

Maxwell, J. (2003). *The 17 indisputable laws of teamwork.* Nashville, TN: Thomas Nelson.

Mondale, S., & Patton, S. B. (2001). *School: The story of American public education.* Boston: Beacon Press.

Palmer, P. J. (1998). *The courage to teach.* San Francisco: Jossey-Bass.

Peterson, K. D. (2002, April). *The professional development of principals: Innovations and opportunities.* Paper commissioned for the first meeting of the National Commission for the Advancement of Educational Leadership Preparation, Racine, WI.

Senge, P. (1990). *The fifth discipline: The art and practice of the learning organization.* New York: Doubleday/Currency.

CHAPTER TWO

Shaping Campus Culture

A vision without a task is a dream. A task without a vision is
drudgery. But a task with vision can change the world.
—*Black Elk (as cited in Blaydes, 2003, p. 107)*

To see a picture of culture, look at the flag of India. You will see a
symbol of a wheel. When the country of India was created, there were
more than 500 principalities that became a part of the one state. According
to Noah benShea (2003), "To be a spoke in the Indian wheel means to be
part of something large, a part that makes the whole work, makes the
wheel turn" (p. 142). In this way, culture is what shapes what we are as well
as what we think; it is the way we communicate, the way we interact, and
what we value (Pang, 2005). All of these pieces fitting together create the
culture. Culture is the way we have school.

Several research studies have shown a relationship between school
culture and achievement. For example, Fullan (1999) identified school
culture as critical to improving teaching and learning. Another study by
Newmann and associates (1996) found that schools were successful when
their cultures emphasized student learning, high expectations, and support for innovation. Understanding this connection is a major component
in the leader's vision for a successful school. After all, as baseball player
Yogi Berra said, "If you don't know where you are, you might not be there"
(as cited in Blaydes, 2003, p. 134).

Envisioning a successful school culture is only the beginning in
shaping a positive school culture. This is why Matthews and Crow (2003)
suggested that before principals can improve the tasks of teaching and

learning in schools, they must first understand the school's culture. In other words, principals must view the school from a much larger perspective than they had as classroom teachers.

Although the culture of the school captures the identity of the school, the *climate* refers to patterns of behavior that manifest that culture. Research emphasizes that understanding change processes directed at the school climate are necessary for successful principals to lead in shaping a positive, affirming campus culture in which student learning thrives (Deal & Peterson, 1999). Embedded in the artifacts, beliefs, rituals, activities, and expectations at the school are evidences of the school's culture. Therefore, principals must spend time identifying and understanding the culture that exists, and they must have a clear vision of the school culture to be developed.

Because culture is embedded in a multiplicity of ways in all that we do at school, the practices principals shared for shaping campus culture are diverse and varied. In shaping a positive, achievement-oriented campus culture, principal James Wells pointed out that shaping campus culture is critical to the success of the school. Most principals rarely have the opportunity to create a campus culture; instead, they inherit an existing culture, and their job becomes one of shaping and reinventing. But James Wells had the opportunity to open a brand-new school, which became a Blue Ribbon middle school, and he is now at an established high school with dramatically changing demographics. Therefore, he has an especially insightful perspective on a principal's role in shaping campus culture.

Building on the research to create positive school cultures, Anthony Ferreira believes that "the development of trust is crucial," whereas Tommy Floyd and Brent Curtice emphasize building strong relationships with the community. Other important parts of the culture wheel are addressed by our award-winning principals, including Manette Schaller's reminder of the importance that a sense of humor plays in shaping a positive school culture.

TRUST IS THE FOUNDATION

Anthony Ferreira
Rehoboth, Massachusetts

The development of trust is crucial to the school's culture, school improvement, and the foundation on which a healthy school community functions. Leaders who motivate people to authentic and lasting changes model behaviors that are important to them each day and are consistent in what they say and do. The trust of a faculty and staff is earned through our behaviors. We all know leaders who tell people what they want to hear rather than the truth. We know people who pay lip service to issues and concerns and never follow through. Principals need to display congruence in their words and actions.

Leadership is often thought of by practitioners in terms of action. Leaders act and point the way. They make strong arguments, motivate people, plan and organize, and see plans through to completion. They encourage, exhort, cajole, and sometimes threaten. We think about what we need to do but can neglect the effects our daily presence means to accomplishing our goals and developing trust.

The kinds of things principals need to do to develop trust range from simple and interpersonal to complex and buildingwide. When we tell a teacher that extra desks will be sent to his or her crowded classroom, we need to be certain it gets done as soon as possible. This is important to the teacher's working conditions, although it is perhaps a relatively small matter to us. When we hear at a faculty meeting that many teachers are concerned about conduct in the cafeteria, we had better follow up promptly after saying we will investigate or address the issue. Trust is earned when we listen to concerns and make earnest and prompt efforts to address them.

Principals earn trust in other ways. When we tell staff that money is tight, we should not be buying that new chair for our office. When different staff members approach us individually about an issue, we should be consistent in what we say to each. If principals can tolerate differing viewpoints and ideas without disparaging those who offer them, we earn the trust and respect of everyone and foster a more open climate.

When we earn the trust of our faculty and staff, we can lead more effectively in all aspects of our work. There will always be differing viewpoints and disagreements about issues in a school. But when disagreements occur, principals who have the trust of their staff will continue to have their respect and confidence.

TEAM THORNTON

James Wells
Houston, Texas

I had the wonderful opportunity to open a new junior high school, Thornton Junior High School, 13 years ago. From the start, I had the advantage of being able to conceptualize the school. Initially, I went out into the community to interface with parents, students, and community members from the two junior highs that would be losing certain neighborhoods and sending them to us. I engaged them in dialogue, and I was able to get ample feedback about what type of school the community wanted.

One thing that became evident was that the parents and students of these communities wanted an open-door policy and a school that welcomed them. Many of the communities were lower income, and the parents felt they were disenfranchised and had no real influence in their children's education at their previous schools (one in particular). There was also a lot of resentment because many of the students had attended a junior high school that had a high percentage of high-socioeconomic-status, advantaged students who were allowed to remain at the school. This school had been twice designated as a National Blue Ribbon School, and as is usual with boundary decisions, there was resentment from those who had to move toward those who got to stay.

Public Relations Campaign

As a new principal from the beginning, I realized the importance of putting certain mechanisms in place to combat these issues. I began a public relations campaign, capitalizing on a beautiful new facility and creating a colorful pamphlet that began to get people excited. Although we were in a remote part of the district (many parents would have to drive three times farther than their previous neighborhood schools), the physical plant was state of the art. However, physical surroundings alone do not determine the quality of a school.

Find the Right Staff

I began relentlessly pursuing the best, most talented staff I could possibly acquire. To this day, I still believe that one of the principal's most critical functions is that of gatekeeper. A school will only be as good as the people you allow to walk through the door (this includes those who do not fit the school's philosophy, and therefore leave through that same door). If you are able to hire 7 or 8 out of 10 people who support the philosophy and goals of the organization, incredible things happen. If you are successful only 5 out of 10 times, you are going to have problems, because your critical mass (on your faculty) will be hard to identify or move when you need to do so for reform's sake, support of goals or programs, and so forth.

Hire Tough

The first lesson I learned was to hire tough. That means interviewing three, five, or as many as eight prospects for each position to be filled! It sounds like a lot of work, but as long as the applicant pool has qualified individuals that fit your school's philosophy and mission, you will find them. Which brings me to the next point, in keeping with effective school correlates thinking—you must have a clearly defined mission and clear goals. These were established collaboratively with our new staff and our parent groups from the beginning. Our mission statement was a reflection of the best of everyone's thinking about what this school would be, and we resolved that in five years (the first time we would be eligible), we too would have a Blue Ribbon school.

Team Spirit

Out of this, the attitude of "Team Thornton" was born. This collaborative mind-set pervaded every facet of our school, as it was founded on the basis of a team culture. Using the Carnegie Foundation's *Turning Points 2000* report (Jackson & Davis, 2000), we configured our teaching teams into small learning communities located in distinct areas of the building (pods) that had distinct identities. Our teachers had common planning periods for their interdisciplinary teams in their pod areas (i.e., math, science, social studies, reading, and language arts), and each teacher also had a planning period with each of his or her content teams to ensure that there was continuity in the curriculum, sharing of resources, and so forth. Every facet of the school had a distinct role in the overall Team Thornton concept, and our parents and community were an important part of this team.

Engage Parents

We adopted the motto, "None of us is as smart as all of us." Realizing the importance of parents and community members in shaping the culture of the school, we worked hard to engage parents in every way possible.

Each Thornton Patriot team—the Minutemen, Pioneers, Trailblazers, and so forth—had team parents who came daily to help facilitate the needs of their respective groups. In addition, as a part of the overall Volunteers in Public Schools (VIPS) program, we did everything possible to get parents involved. We had a "brown bag" program that allowed parents to take certain types of clerical work home so they could volunteer during nonschool hours, we provided a VIPS room that was equipped with a computer and toys for young children so parents could bring them with them and yet still volunteer for certain tasks, and we also had a monthly nighttime meeting with the parents to provide a forum for questions and discussions. We sometimes would present topics of interest to stay connected. This was a way to keep our finger on the pulse of the community.

We had potluck suppers for any and all families who wanted to attend. We would always have some of our student groups perform on these occasions. This was a great way to get to know the parents and community better. We not only had standard open houses, but we also allowed our parents to attend school one day a year with their student to experience firsthand what each student experienced. (We had as many as 500 in attendance!)

Parent involvement and teamwork were critically important in our culture. Although these examples are by no means all inclusive, they are indicative of the level of trust that our parents had in our staff. Parents definitely knew they were welcomed and, in fact, very much needed. And this was a mutual arrangement, as the parents were instrumental in helping us to achieve our goal as a National Blue Ribbon School of Excellence in 2000. Often, we had outside visitors comment on the harmonious tone of our environment, where everyone seemed to connect in some way.

Culture Is Observable

Five minutes of observation to the casual observer in the lobby area of a school or organization can tell you a lot about what that organization values. Our culture was based on the belief that no matter where our kids came from or what their educational deficits were, our staff would find a way to make them successful. This attitude goes back to my original comments about finding enough of the right people to bring into the organization to have a critical mass, a preponderance of people who value the same things, agree on the same goals, and synergize to accomplish them.

Ongoing Staff Development

Part of the culture at Thornton was a direct result of our ongoing staff development emphasis. From the beginning, to meet the needs of our diverse learners (we were approximately 60% minority and almost 30% economically disadvantaged, with a high at-risk percentage), we focused on learning styles, higher-order thinking skills, brain-based learning, quadrant personality theory (advocating congruency in learning styles and teaching styles), and writing across the content areas, reading across the content areas, and others. Using quadrant personality theory also helped us develop even stronger teaching teams.

We did not believe in a "flavor of the month" staff development approach, as we continued to scaffold our staff development each year, maintaining a focus on where we had been; introducing new strategies, practices, and bases of knowledge; and continually going back and bringing new people up to date each year. Probably one of the strongest areas of our Blue Ribbon application was in the area of staff development.

One last note in regard to affecting the school culture in the area of staff development: I taught most if not all staff development with the help of various other staff members. It is so important for the principal to be perceived as an effective teacher, interested and knowledgeable in the areas of instructional improvement. Generally, this is more common at lower levels like middle school and elementary school. Staff development is the lifeblood of your instructional program and helps to shape and perpetuate your culture!

Our kids at Thornton did remarkably well, and their achievement was always at or very near the recognized level of performance in the state's Academic Excellence Indicator System (AEIS) system. Thornton received many other acknowledgments for having outstanding staff and programs. The staff and parents believed in our kids, and Thornton had one of the most dedicated staff, most supportive group of parents, and best reputations around.

INFLUENCING THE SCHOOL CULTURE

Tommy Floyd
Somerset, Kentucky

When you become a principal, you inherit a staff, a community, students, and many expectations. Change does not come quickly, so expect resistance! You will have to sell your ideas! Assess all that is positive and negative, then fight all that is negative and build on all that is positive. Never spend lots of time talking about the negatives; never stop talking about the positives!

What you make a priority is and will always be a priority. Follow up, follow up, follow up! Most battles are won and lost simply on how persistent you are; nothing important or worthwhile happens quickly.

Remember the importance of working with the community to build a strong, positive school culture. The following best practices contribute to this goal:

- Wear the media out with what is going on in your school—make it sound exciting; it will be! The media needs positive news; give them some.
- Paint a picture of success in all areas: curricular, extracurricular, faculty, staff, and students.
- Always find a way to be positive with the media. They buy ink by the barrel, and, yes, people read what they print. Find reporters who like to cover school news; seek a professional understanding with them. A positive relationship with them will pay huge dividends in public relations.
- Become your own public relations spokesperson; attend every function offered to show off students. The people you show students to will be more likely to sponsor programs when they see the students recognized. Everyone wants to be on a winning team!
- Find out what your community needs: facility, training, student preparation requests, job skills, and more.
- Seek partnerships in labs, teams, fundraisers, job opportunities, and teacher enhancement. The community loves to feel that it is a part of establishing the school culture.
- Never assume that what you or your school decides to do is not discussed at supper, at church, at meetings, at bridge tables, and on the golf course. Most of the time, common sense will prevail. Stick with it!

SHAPING A DEMOGRAPHICALLY CHANGING HIGH SCHOOL

James Wells
Houston, Texas

School culture supersedes everything we do. The best-planned curriculum and best-trained teachers in the world can be undermined if you do not make a conscious effort to define and evaluate your culture, striving to create an environment that meets the needs of your staff, students, parents, and community. I have had the good fortune to start (no one can create a culture, only influence its direction as it takes on a life of its own) a cultural evolution in a new school (Thornton Middle School) and watch it take shape, and then to inherit a school with an established culture and be faced with the task of changing certain aspects of that culture for the benefit of the kids. The school with the challenging demographic change is where I am currently principal, Cypress Creek High School.

Cypress Creek High School opened in 1976 and has graduated 26 classes since then. Over the years, Cy-Creek has been one of the top schools in the Cypress Fairbanks School District and in the state. However, like all schools, it is beginning to mirror district, state, and national trends demographically. Now, in 2005, Cy-Creek is approximately 59% white, 25% Hispanic, 9% African American, and 7% other. Still, last year's senior class received $16 million in scholarships, and $14.5 million of that was for academics alone. This set a school and district record. Of the 581 graduates, 57% planned to attend a four-year college or university, 30% planned on attending a two-year college, and 12% planned on entering the military, going to vocational or technical schools, or entering the world of work. We had 12 National Merit finalists!

In addition, Cy-Creek has one of the highest advanced placement (AP) participation rates in the state and nation. In 2002–2003, it made *Newsweek Magazine's* list as one of the most challenging schools in America based on its AP participation rate. I cite these examples to illustrate the paradoxical nature of Cy-Creek's student body. Although it has been rated as exemplary and recognized in the state's AEIS system in the past, it has not done so for five years because of the increased challenges of changing demographics. It still maintains some of the highest overall scores in the district in some areas and is much higher than state averages, but there is an obvious achievement gap when you disaggregate the data from various subgroups. There is an obvious difference between the highest performers and African American, economically disadvantaged, and Hispanic subgroups.

In terms of the existing culture that I experienced as Cy-Creek's new principal in 2002–2003, the staff has been challenged because of the student body demographic shifting. Although there are still a remarkable number of high achievers, there are a growing number of students who are in need of a more responsive way of teaching to bring them up to an acceptable level of performance. This challenge is hard for many to understand, as many still envision the same school that Cy-Creek presented 5 to

10 years ago. Although we want to retain the aspect of the school culture that challenges students to a rigorous program, we must accept that we are failing to provide all students an equitable education.

This challenge is so different from the one called for in opening a new school with a clean slate and the ability to orchestrate a culture to accomplish accepted goals. Therefore, I am slowly working in areas of staff development, emphasizing many proven staff development strategies, including how to respect learner differences, getting away from a one-size-fits-all approach to teaching, working on energizing lessons with brain-based strategies, learning how to differentiate instruction, and so forth. In terms of our staff development program, it is a work in progress, and, slowly, we are working to change the mind-set of our staff to more accurately reflect the learning needs of all of our students while maintaining the best of the "elitist attitude" that has promoted a very competitive school and community culture.

Staff Relations

In terms of staff relations, our Building Better Relationships committee members have done a lot. I meet with them frequently to explore ways, incentives, and so forth to enhance staff morale, attendance, communication, teamwork, and attitudes. I make it a personal challenge to stay connected to the staff in the same manner as I do the students.

Visibility and Availability

Visibility and availability are critically important, so I subscribe to the old school philosophy of "management while wandering around," doing hall monitoring and frequent classroom drop-in visits as well as formal evaluation observations. It is important that the principal is viewed as involved in the day-to-day rhythms of a campus, and his or her presence and availability to kids and staff exudes the message "I care about you and this school."

The adage that "we monitor what we value" applies as well. It is amazing how many positive interactions even one walk around the campus yields with staff and students. It is also amazing how many problems you can note and solve. It's a great opportunity to energize oneself and also keep one's finger on the pulse of the school. Informal conversations and simple observations are extremely reliable measures. I think visibility and accessibility are at the top of teachers' lists in evaluating a principal's commitment level. People first; then, of all the other myriad responsibilities that come with the job, the greatest is to ensure student success, which can be gauged through countless measures.

Support the Total School Program

It is also important to support the total school program. My philosophy has always been that if you see evidence of a strong fine arts program with evidence of student performance and visual displays of students' talents, this indicates the heart and soul of the school. Kids derive their sense of belonging and self-identities from their affiliations, and fine arts participation creates better human beings. It serves as a great equalizer and adds meaning to the school experience for a lot of students. A well-rounded, comprehensive high school program is more than about strong athletic programs, and it is possible for even athletes to seek the enrichment fine arts programs provide. Much of this can be influenced by the principal in the way programs are supported and acknowledged.

Strong Communication

I also believe a strong communication network is necessary to maintain a culture of trust. Any time an event happens that is of any serious consequence involving a student incident or community problem, staff members resent finding out through the informal network. Consequently, I make a concerted effort to keep them informed through an emergency e-mail process or a faculty meeting.

Faculty meetings are an important part of the school culture, and we have one per grading period. The purpose is to celebrate the end of the grading period and successes, to disseminate information, and to develop a common sense of purpose and unity. We always start out with a student group from one of the fine arts performance groups (choir, orchestra, band, theater, or art display). We conduct our business—many times I use humor or some type of energetic approach to make points and lighten things up—and we always make room for acknowledgments, appreciations, and affirmations. This involves staff members standing and delivering public praise of some sort for a colleague or sharing good news about the success of a program or students.

Faculty Awards

Afterward, we award our six Top Cat awards to individuals who have been peer nominated by a colleague for their dedication to student success. Their pictures are placed in the lounge, and they are given an attractive trophy as a reminder to be kept in their classroom for six weeks. We end our meetings with several prize drawings, usually area restaurant gift certificates solicited by the Building Better Relations group.

Figure 2.1   Catch of the Week—James Wells's Weekly Message to Staff and Faculty

---

How many of you remember Clint Eastwood as Dirty Harry and his now famous utterance, "Go ahead, make my day!" Well, most of us have a slightly different view of what it takes to pick us up or energize us. We don't have to shoot anyone to have that happen! I want to take this opportunity to make a Cougar staff member's day for a notable honor. Marlene Lobberecht continues to set the standard for professional educators. Among the many accolades and achievements that she has accomplished, add another one. Marlene began serving her term in June as the president for the Texas Association for Family and Consumer Sciences. She also recently received commendations for her inservice contribution to the district's Early Childhood Professions teachers and her presentation on the Iowa State University campus in Ames, Iowa, this summer.

If you know of any notable achievements or honors either you or any of your colleagues have recently accomplished, go ahead and "make their day" by letting me know so they can be properly acknowledged. Often, we have many of our staff and students doing absolutely incredible things, but no one notices, so let's make a point to acknowledge each other (students and staff) in a variety of ways. I would also like to mention that we are finalizing a list of campus awards and accomplishments to be produced in pamphlet form and to be posted on our campus Web site under the Cougar Kudos section. This section will include staff and student acknowledgments from last year. We currently get approximately 4,000 to 5,000 hits on this site from all over the world! If you did not respond to Jo Winn's request for submissions, please do so as soon as possible. We don't want to take for granted the wonderful things you and our students have accomplished in the last year. Go ahead, make our day! Have a great week.

Catch of the Week

Another thing I do as a principal to create a positive climate for staff is the "Catch of the Week" communication to all staff. This is a great way to stay in touch, give reminders and updates, re-emphasize staff development, give encouragement, and most important, acknowledge outstanding achievements by staff members. I call it the Catch of the Week because of our emphasis on the FISH philosophy (see Figure 2.1).

Other ways I acknowledge staff include

- Personalized birthday cards with individual messages and a complimentary lunch for each staff member.
- Cougar Pride awards (certificates as a special appreciation for a job well done, commendation, etc.).
- "Defending Your Den" certificates for any teacher doing a great job monitoring between classes. These can be given by any administrator, and the teacher's name is entered into a monthly drawing

for a day off. The administrative team (including me) teach the teacher's classes. They love this one!

- Spirit Day every Friday. Staff wear a staff shirt, jeans, and tennis shoes. We often award extra jean days for rewards. We have a very formal dress code usually, so they love this one as well.

More Communication

As in any organization, there will always be the need to address concerns and problems. Schools are social systems with formal and informal networks. Many times, there are concerns and problems that are talked about through the informal network, and often, misconceptions prevail. We have a Cougar Pulse committee composed of one representative from each facet of the school. It is an advisory committee that brings written (anonymous optional) concerns regarding an array of topics, from no toilet paper in the faculty restroom to dissatisfaction with the grading policy. A submission must also be accompanied with a proposed solution. This is not a "gripe" committee, and often proposed resolutions are adopted, policy is reviewed, or action is taken. It empowers staff and gives faculty a voice. There are one counselor, assistant principal, and director of instruction who also serve. The committee is a great safety outlet and helps keep the informal network in check.

Personal Connections

We have a "5 to 10" rule. This was an outgrowth of the FISH philosophy training and the numerous suggestions that we solicited from staff members on ways to improve our environment and make the school a pleasant place. The rule is, if you are 5 feet away from someone, greet them verbally, and if you are 10 feet away, acknowledge nonverbally. I do this with all students in the building. It takes a conscious effort but is very worthwhile, as it really speaks volumes to them.

Another aspect of our campus staff development focus is Ruby Payne's (1996) work dealing with children of poverty, and Magnificent Seven training, which advocates teaching strategies for dealing with students from diverse backgrounds.

Capturing Kids' Hearts is another program that empowers teachers. It is almost a social skills approach for teachers and adults in the school setting to break down barriers and gain a mutual trust (i.e., teachers stand at their door and shake every student's hand, use affirmations in class, etc.). It is so imperative that adults in the high school setting are trusted by students as genuinely interested in them as individuals. The old adage

"They don't care how much you know, until they know how much you care" is so true of kids. If every adult in the school subscribes to this philosophy, it can transform your campus.

Student Body Relations

Student relations are as important as staff relations for the principal. There are many best practices that I implement to create positive student relationships. For example, every week I do a *Principal's Minute* (see Figure 2.2).

Visit With Senior Class

I visit with every senior English class at length to talk about topics like living up to one's full potential, avoiding "senioritis," the importance of parents, integrity and the importance of not cheating, avoiding bad decisions, and so forth. I make this a campy talk with a lot of animation and humor. I use a lot of quotes and poignant real-life examples as well. It has really paid great dividends in letting the kids know who their principal is and about expectations, but most important, that I care about each of them and their success. I talk to the seniors this way because they are campus leaders and can set the tone for the student body. We have had incredible, well-behaved senior classes over the last three years! I talk to other small groups of underclassmen throughout the year, but not as extensively. Senior talks are done at the beginning of the year. I also meet regularly with student council officers and talk with other organizations to get input and promote community service. Connection, connection, connection—this is so important for a principal.

Recognitions

I do continuous student recognitions, individually and collectively through my *Principal's Minute*, the school Web site, parent newsletters, and faculty meetings—any way possible. These kids have done remarkable things for years. They are so talented, and they can be taken for granted. Celebrate! Celebrate! Celebrate their successes. Make them feel special.

I send our Cougar Pride Awards to students for a number of accomplishments, school related or not. They can be for achievement, effort, or good citizenship. Other staff members do so as well. The student receives a certificate with his or her name and reason for nomination. The student's name is entered in a weekly drawing. We have 15 to 20 winners each week who then receive a free pizza. You guessed it—the kids love it! On Thursdays,

Figure 2.2   James Wells's Weekly *Principal's Minute*

Good Morning, Cougars!

Since the public address and bell systems were not functioning yesterday, I did not get a chance to officially welcome you back on the first day of school. We are so very pleased to be welcoming our returning students as well as many new faces in the crowd. We hope you had a relaxing, productive summer and are ready to be back. Your teachers and the Cy-Creek staff have worked hard in anticipation of your return and are excited about the new year. We hope you are, too. You might note that there are some obvious, as well as subtle, changes in the Cy-Creek environment, as we had many renovation projects going on this summer, including a complete replacement of the air conditioning and heating systems. As a result, there will continue to be fine tuning of the HVAC system, as well as the bells and intercom, and building clean-up efforts will be taking place over the next several days. We apologize for any inconveniences and appreciate the way you responded to the challenges yesterday.

As you begin a new school year, I would like for you to take a moment to answer this question: Why am I here at Cy-Creek this year? Hopefully, you will give this some serious thought and commit your answer to memory or write it down somewhere. I would imagine most of you (hopefully) would be mentioning, in your answer, your goals for the future. Remember, the beginning is half of every action, so just being here is a great start.

The beginning of each school year also presents a clean slate, an opportunity for you to start anew, moving toward your goals. Another thought about beginning I would like to share with you comes from a famous British author, George Eliot: "It's never too late to be what you might have been." Think about that. This new year presents numerous opportunities for you. Hopefully, by year's end, you will have taken advantage of what your teachers have offered you—a chance to be successful in your coursework. And hopefully, you will also be involved in Cy-Creek High School in some way, through extracurricular, club, or service-oriented activities. There is an abundance of opportunities awaiting you, opportunities that, through your collective involvement, will make Cy-Creek an even greater school and will make your school experience more enjoyable. So, I encourage you to get involved.

Over the next several days, your teachers will be orienting you to the new year. Please keep in mind that the first two weeks of school generally involve leveling classes, taking care of scheduling problems, and establishing routines. Mr. Gordon, our associate principal, will be going over several details with you regarding this.

One final item: It's important to note that schools, to function for the good of all, must have norms of behavior and guidelines. It is imperative that each of you review the Code of Conduct and sign the Code of Conduct acknowledgment form to do your part to keep Cypress Creek a safe and productive learning environment. Your teachers will begin reviewing this information with you beginning today. Superseding our Code of Conduct is a much simpler code that we prominently display in the cafeteria, the Cougar Creed. We should each strive to live by this creed as a part of the Cougar team (teachers/faculty and students). The creed requires each of us to

- Try to improve daily.
- Exhibit respect to self and others.
- Accept responsibility for actions.
- Make a daily effort to communicate honestly.
- Be a team player.

I hope that you had a great first day of school and that you have answered the rhetorical question, "Why am I here this year at Cy-Creek?" And now, for the first time this year, I'll close with "You just can't hide that Cougar Pride!"

---

the front lobby reeks of pizza delivered from Mr. Gatti's at lunchtime. I pay for this out of the activity account, and it is a great investment.

Promoting Citizenship

In promoting citizenship and social skills, we have the Cougar Challenge every Monday during our advisory class, a 30-minute homeroom period that is coupled with fourth-hour classes before or after lunch. The topics are diverse but always focus on some social skill aspect. The lesson and ensuing discussion are generally 15 to 20 minutes but often last the whole period. Lessons and materials are prepared ahead of time and given to staff. We feel this program has also added to our school culture, as it reinforces certain values and expectations at Cy-Creek.

Our students are extremely responsive when it comes to service learning and community service projects. They have shown to be kind and generous, and we promote this on our campus. You would not believe the number of relief efforts and activities that took place over the days after Hurricane Katrina. The 2004 tsunami disaster was no different. Every organization and club is doing something, and it is all coordinated by our student council. We have a "Portrait of a Cy Fair Graduate" in our district that describes all of the attributes and qualities we want our students to depart with. The "Responsible Citizen" dimension is an important one that needs to be cultivated, which includes showing compassion for others.

THEME-BASED EDUCATION: THE HIGH SCHOOL'S MANTRA

Sharon Toriello
Kinnelon, New Jersey

The best practice that I want to share is our theme-based education. After soliciting suggestions from faculty, students, and parents at the conclusion of a school year, a broad-based theme is selected by the administrative team of the high school to anchor attitudes, initiatives, and defined goals for the next school year. That theme becomes our mantra for the year.

When students enter the building on the very first day of school, every showcase and every corridor bulletin board is decorated with this theme.

Every mailing, every letter home to parents and students, T-shirts on the opening day of school, every faculty agenda, every newsletter, and the outside community billboard—all of these showcase our theme for the year. All professional efforts are directed at translating that mantra in tangible, specific ways. Specific themes that we have used in the past four years are

2003–2004	It's all about commitment
2002–2003	The power of pride
2001–2002	Make a connection—Build a bridge
2000–2001	Respect—Celebrate the gift

The following are ways that we have implemented these themes.

It's All About Commitment

Our commitment for this year was to academic achievement, to extracurricular life, to volunteerism, to a drug- and alcohol-free school, to peer-to-peer sensitivity through an anti-bullying consciousness, to professional development, to professional evaluation methods, to technology education, and to enhanced public relations. These commitments are directly linked to both formal and informal strategic planning at our district and campus levels.

Teachers were asked to craft classroom-based commitments for the students. Students suggested and designed new initiatives for our high school to consider what would require significant commitment and a measure of "giving back." One of these initiatives was Volunteer Kids, a totally student-driven effort to organize and mobilize a cadre of high school students to assess community needs and link volunteers to those needs. Approximately 35 students were on board as of this writing.

In addition, a group of students is working with a faculty volunteer to organize students in support of Habitat for Humanity. Our hope as administrative leaders is to encourage a culture in our school in which students develop an understanding of the need for commitment and of the need to get outside of oneself and give back to others in the process.

The Power of Pride

To honor the high school's 40th anniversary, the concept of pride in our accomplishments anchored school year 2002–2003. The entire school reconnected to the highlights of 1963. An all–high school exhibition culminated the year, complete with student recitals, projects, and performance-based assessments. Former employees, alumni, dignitaries, and the entire community were solicited through formal invitation to return to our high school and celebrate 40 years of pride.

Make a Connection—Build a Bridge

In 2001–2002, we committed to strengthening connections on all levels of school life. We used the logo of bridges all year long. Some ways that we built stronger bridges in our high school were

- Totally reassessing our transition process to ninth grade from middle school. This resulted in a structured, multifaceted program including middle school and high school department areas, child study team personnel, counselors, parents, and of course, students.
- Establishing a principal's ambassador program. A group of hand-selected, nonelected students were invited to serve as advisors to the principal to ensure that all student voices were being heard, in addition to student council members and class officers.
- Establishing specific articulation initiatives between high school and middle school.
- Including students at "Home and School" meetings.
- Building new partnerships with community groups to support each others' efforts, such as the Center for Lifelong Learning.
- Fine-tuning the Administrative/Faculty Roundtable to ensure responsible communication in an open forum.

Respect—Celebrate the Gift

Our high school has a Spirit Week each year that culminates in a gala football half-time show for homecoming. All four classes are challenged to create a huge banner, selecting an appropriate message to the school community from that class. The banners are unveiled at halftime through class presentations and then are evaluated by a team of judges. All four banners hang in our gymnasium for the rest of the school year. During 2000–2001, each class embraced the schoolwide mantra of respect as the universal song of Spirit Week. I was proud that every banner focused on respect in a different context: cultural diversity, relationships, country, and family values. The entire evening underscored the mantra of pride. This was especially gratifying, to say the least, as Spirit Week is a communitywide tradition, greeted with passion each year.

At Kinnelon High School, we believe that broad-based themes help frame the yearly journey toward meeting goals. When these themes link to goals in specific ways, then our students begin to find meaning in the words spoken from the podium of adults. The themes become theirs, as does the work that defines them.

Developing a Professional Learning Community

Manette Schaller
Houston, Texas

As a campus, as well as a district, our focus is on becoming a professional learning community. We believe that the essential three questions in DuFour and Eaker's (1998) book are the foundation to establish best practices for the campus. What is it we want all students to learn? Basically, in Texas, we want them to know the Texas Essential Knowledge and Skills. How will we know that students are learning? We learn this through assessment. What will we do when they do not learn the content initially? This question causes us to put on our thinking caps, be creative, and work in collaboration to see what else we can do to assist students in the learning process. We tend to operate from a possibilities-unlimited mentality. To help this happen, at Alief Taylor High School, we provided staff development for our teachers. We also met with department chairs and subject leaders and used the *Handbook for Smart School Teams* by Anne Cozemius and Jan O'Neill (2002) as a guide.

It is important for students, parents, and staff to come together and have a shared vision and mission. As educators, we must be persistent and purposeful in what we do. Communication and collaboration are essential to the overall success of a campus. I would like to believe that what sets our campus apart is not so much what we do but how we do it.

Not only do we focus on the traditional three Rs, but on the Schaller 3 Rs: reflection, relentlessness, and relationships. As leaders, we must model taking time to reflect on data and best practices, and personally—as

Stephen Covey (1989) said, to "sharpen the saw"—do something to take care of ourselves. We must teach our students to reflect on the work that they are doing and allow time during the school day for all parties to have time to reflect. It is important that subject teams have common planning periods so they can collaborate, address the DuFour and Eaker (1998) questions, develop common assessments, and review data. We built our master schedule so that, for example, all Algebra I teachers have a common planning period on A days, all English I teachers have a common planning period, and so on. This has worked well for the core subjects. We also have been able to do this for theater and dance, and we are working to get more electives with common planning periods.

It is also extremely important that an atmosphere of trust be developed to allow for meaningful conversations. One thing that we did to develop this atmosphere of trust was to let the teachers know that our campus administration did not subscribe to the "gotcha" mentality. When we look at data, we are looking to see how our students are performing and what practices are successful in the classroom. It is important for us as a staff to realize that the more we share, the more successful our students will be. Again, the center of all conversations must be on students and student achievement. This fosters a very positive campus climate.

Furthermore, we must be relentless in our commitment to our profession; our students deserve nothing less. As educators, we must be committed on a daily basis to doing whatever it takes to allow our students to succeed personally and academically. Their future depends on it. We must establish meaningful relationships with our students. We must know their interests and goals. We must also share about ourselves with the students. We do several things to build relationships with our students. For example, our teachers call each student in their advisory prior to the start of school to welcome them to Taylor and the coming school year. When I called a group of freshmen, several did not believe that I was the principal calling. They thought a friend was pulling a prank on them. It was precious! I also meet with students once a month. We call this group Lion Leadership, and it includes representatives from various clubs and organizations. The meeting is open to everyone, and often, many students just come to see what is happening on the campus.

In closing, as educators, in addition to everything already mentioned thus far, we must have a sense of humor. We also must have a strong support network. It is imperative to keep a special folder with notes from staff, students, and parents. When you have a tough day, which will happen, you can pull out a note that will truly touch your heart and be reminded why you do what you do. According to Elsie Lewis Bailey, principal of Booker T. High School in Memphis, Tennessee, "As education leaders, we dream, we do, we care." That's a great start for sustaining leadership. Oprah Winfrey (2004) shared, "Listen. Pay attention. Treasure every moment." As an educator, I listen, I pay attention, and I know for sure that I treasure every moment as principal of Alief Taylor High School.

SHAPING THROUGH PROFESSIONAL DEVELOPMENT

Stewart Carey
Westfield, New Jersey

Roosevelt Intermediate School's professional development begins with organized recruiting, interviewing, and hiring. We work diligently to find teachers who are well prepared, who are thoroughly trained, and who have a solid understanding of their content area before hiring. They must be passionate about early adolescent students and willing to grow and learn as professionals. As a result, the professional staff at Roosevelt comes to the job with a commitment to middle-level education and a thorough understanding of the content area.

New staff members have a week-long, middle-level orientation program in August at which they get to know the school community, our curriculum, their colleagues, and the expectations of instruction in the Westfield Public Schools. A districtwide New Teacher Institute is ongoing for two years. It provides workshops, training, and professional development for new teachers.

Our school district also offers afterschool professional development workshops for all teachers, which include differentiated instruction, collaboration with community groups, technology, and special education. Department supervisors hold monthly meetings in which relevant topics in curriculum are discussed. Teachers routinely share effective instructional techniques, review curriculum revisions, and discuss ways to improve our program.

Finally, faculty meetings provide professional development, in which teachers share ideas on differentiated instruction, collaborate about improving our program, and share ideas that work to enhance student achievement. Informally, teachers freely share their ideas, support one another, and work diligently to ensure that every student is making academic progress and that our program is continually improving.

It Takes a Village

Brent Curtice
Paonia, Colorado

"It takes a village to raise a child" has become such a cliché, but in Paonia, Colorado, which is small and rural, parents and the schools have always relied on the community to develop and to enrich our youth. I have been accused of always looking at the world through rose-colored glasses, but I strongly believe that our students are in good hands, as long as we make relationships our primary focus. When someone influential in your life believes in you, you will always make an extra effort to rise to the occasion. We must make fostering relationships the number one priority in education, as our children face innumerable challenges. If we can make them confident that they can rise to the occasion and do whatever is necessary to make their lives and our world better, we will have succeeded.

Our students face a constantly evolving world with information doubling or tripling every 10 years. Our task is to give them the tools to learn how to learn, to teach them where and how to access the information that they need, and to give them the curiosity to seek innovations and positive change. As educators, we must nurture students' belief that they are competent and fully capable of meeting future challenges, even if they fail. Through failure, much can be learned, but we must also teach persistence and the belief that nothing worthwhile is ever gained without effort and commitment.

Guaranteeing a Better Future for the Entire Community

Dan Stepenosky
Beverly Hills, California

Beverly Hills High School (BHHS) serves a diverse population of students. Approximately 22.6% of our students are foreign born. These students come to us from 49 foreign countries, such as Iran, Korea, Israel, Russia, and the Ukraine. Nearly 47% of our students have a home language other than English. In addition, in agreement with the Los Angeles Unified School District, BHHS accepts up to 150 out-of-district, ethnically diverse students as part of our diversity program. Multiculturalism in our student body is represented throughout the academic and extracurricular programs.

Outstanding programs such as AP, English learners, special education, performing arts, technical arts, athletics, and a regional occupational program combine with an exemplary core curriculum and reflect the training and talents of the teachers, as well as the remarkable facilities and resources available on campus. Our students have access to hands-on training and performance opportunities in performing arts, architecture, wood sculpting, robotics, broadcasting, journalism, and athletics.

With a student-counselor ratio of 267 to 1, the guidance department at BHHS facilitates an integrated program that consists of academic counseling, guidance curriculum, individualized student planning, and support systems designed to help students steer an appropriate path through high school.

Both the school and the Beverly Hills community understand the connection between the actions of today and the results of tomorrow. Continual self-assessment ensures that "Today Well Lived," the motto of BHHS, applies to every student in our school, and we are aggressively committed to the idea that meeting the needs of every child is our guarantee of a better tomorrow for the entire community.

Shaping a Culture of Leadership in a Rural School

Brent Curtice
Paonia, Colorado

Overseeing a small school in a rural area has provided me the chance to respond to a variety of needs and opportunities. As an administrator,

I strongly support the benefits of an open-door policy, allowing staff, students, and the community the opportunity to freely express individual opinions and concerns. Focusing on good listening skills has created a positive environment in which all concerned feel safe enough to take risks.

Staff development is a priority that encourages teachers to take risks. The more knowledge a person has, the more risks he or she can take. I encourage my staff to "think outside the box" to develop innovative programs, creating enthusiasm and excitement for learning. One such example is Integrated Studies, a three-hour class in which English, science, and social studies are team taught by three different teachers. Individually and cooperatively, students work with community experts to synthesize the material, emphasizing real-world situations and experiments.

I also am a firm believer that I must model continued learning and development. Paonia High School has always been on the cutting edge as far as use of technology, but technology is useless without the knowledge to use it as an educational tool. When I ask staff to learn a new program or new piece of technology, I know that my knowledge of that same information is vital to creating a positive learning environment. If I do not understand what I am asking my staff to master, how can I expect them to use the information that we both expect our students to use? Because we constantly demonstrate our ability to master new technology and be innovative in our use of it in our classrooms, our school district has rewarded us with the newest and best technology available. Better communication that has resulted from the required use of the First Class communications system has created a more positive environment because of increased awareness of all activities, times, and expectations.

During my tenure as principal, we helped facilitate the passage of a bond issue that has created a wonderful physical facility, which has expanded our options for students. The merger of the two staffs and buildings has allowed us to better use both for the benefit of our students. By blending the two staffs, their strengths can be maximized to increase student learning opportunities. For instance, we can now offer junior high school students the opportunity to take a foreign language. The merger has also allowed us to create new courses and expand our science curriculum in both buildings.

Focusing on a more positive environment has additional benefits. A zero tolerance policy toward harassment and bullying has created a safe environment. In the past three years, our attendance has risen from 93% to 96%. Respect toward others has resulted in fewer than 15 out-of-school suspensions a year and zero expulsions. Our standardized state and national test scores have risen, and more of our students are choosing to pursue a higher education.

Through positive relationships and enthusiastic role models, the climate of Paonia High School is conducive to creating feelings of safety and security, allowing students to take risks.

THREE WAYS TO IMPROVE STUDENT ACHIEVEMENT

Carole Hiltman
Esparto, California

People often ask, "What are the three things your staff did to make such a dramatic change in your students' achievement?" The answer they get is that it is not about a particular instruction technique or reading program; it's about creating a truly unified, aligned system that ensures every student, parent, and staff member is required to take responsibility and participate in improving academic achievement and school progress for all students.

Shared Vision

We started with activities that allowed everyone to participate in reaching collective agreement as to our vision, mission, goals, and purpose. Students, parents, and staff collectively shared ideas, reached common agreements based on sound pedagogy, and then wrote plans that led to a system that has built buy-in and capacity.

Standards Based

We then ensured that all parts of our school were linked and truly standards based. We developed standards-based courses of study (not just course outlines) for all subjects and agreed that all classes would be taught at grade level in accordance with state and district standards. Essentially, we eliminated all remedial classes. For example, all eighth graders take algebra, not just advanced students. To accomplish this with students performing several years beyond grade level, we developed a block schedule in which supported reading and math classes are available to all students. For example, eighth graders get 91 minutes of math daily without sacrificing any other curriculum. Support classes are designed to fill achievement gaps for all students. This is also addressed through one-hour afterschool intervention classes held on campus daily. Despite tremendous district budget cutbacks, we retained our late bus to provide transportation so students could attend these classes.

The creation of standards-based assessments and standards-based report cards has ensured that instruction is truly standards based. Instruction is also now more meaningful, and evaluation of student achievement is more relevant. Students and parents have specific knowledge of expectations and standards. This has also been fostered through implementation of promotion requirements, mandatory parental attendance at each child's annual student-led conference, and the development of an individual learning plan for each student in the school.

Data Analysis by Students

Students analyze their own assessment data and progress, write their goals and plans for achieving them, and then monitor their own progress. They present their portfolios, individual learning plans, and so forth to their parents at an annual individual conference. At the end of eighth grade, students participate in exit interviews, in which they reflect on their middle school progress and discuss goals for high school with a panel of parents, teachers, and community members or businesspeople.

SCHOOL VISION AND STRATEGIC PLANNING ARE EXCITING

Kathleen Haworth
North Hollywood, California

Most of my experience has been as principal for Grades K through 8. That experience includes a variety of roles and skills that are used in some capacity on a daily basis. These include setting and creating school vision, program development, finance and facility planning, and staff development, just to name a few. The first thought of working with middle school students did not appeal to me; however, 12 years later, I have become passionate about this age group and the endless programming possibilities that can enrich their lives.

This age is an exciting yet challenging time in a student's educational development. It is a milestone for social, emotional, and physical development as well as rigorous academic demands. The parents of middle- or upper-grade students are also part of the challenge. In many situations, they find themselves as the child's worst enemy and "out of the loop." This is a big change from their children as elementary students who were eager to share every detail of their day and were diligent about bringing home school information in their backpacks. The parents become dependent on and look to the teachers and the school to provide support, direction, and to some extent, the main liaison between themselves and their children.

School vision and strategic planning can be the most exciting for these grades. Assembling a team that understands the adolescent mind is not easy, and there can be a high rate of burnout. It can also be challenging due to the fact that everyone always has his or her own ideas, especially in the parent community. Finding the point of consensus where everyone is in the boat rowing in the same direction takes a fair amount of effort, planning, and listening. The best advice is to allow people to share ideas and take ownership in the program. As principals, our roles need to be those of facilitators and not controllers. Gray becomes a principal's new favorite color with this age group, as rarely is anything black or white and clear cut.

Prior to becoming a school principal, I spent 11 years in the classroom teaching kindergarten, first, and fifth grades, and kindergarten through eighth-grade music. I could not have become an effective school principal without that background and experience in such a variety of grades and subjects. In developing a middle school program, the teacher/parent experience in those years taught me many valuable lessons. These include the importance of effective listening and taking a 360-degree view of each situation, which is extremely necessary when dealing with middle school issues. Those early years of teaching have become the archives and resources that I still use today when looking for solutions. As teachers leave the classrooms to become principals, they will bring those enriched experiences with them as they have their own styles in school leadership.

GOLDEN OPPORTUNITIES

Kevin Fillgrove
Ephrata, Pennsylvania

Recently, I was asked to accept the role as principal of a middle school. After accepting the position, I was asked to change the school culture, which was deemed to have been in much disarray. On my arrival, I recognized that for a period of 14 years, things had drifted. Despite the good-hearted nature of the staff, they were highly unmotivated, and the school climate was not cohesive. At that point, I recognized not merely another issue but an opportunity. I needed a plan that would not only motivate the staff, but bring everyone together with one goal in mind: high student performance. I mapped out a plan and proceeded with it.

I interviewed each staff member individually for 30 minutes, and I asked them four questions:

1. Can you tell me one fact about yourself?

2. What are five things that a principal needs to know about the school?

3. What question would you like to ask me regarding any topic?

4. What is one thing you believe could help you do your job better?

The number of interviews totaled 90, everyone receiving their 30-minute allotted time.

Using the information obtained from these conversations, I began to hone in on commonalities that existed among all the staff. I prioritized concerns that were most important and most prevalent and addressed them first. I also issued a survey to staff members, identifying levels of collegiality, support, and other related factors. I began implementing various strategies as needed.

One such strategy that I created was the "Golden Star" award. As I mentioned, staff morale and motivation were at low levels, so I specifically used this approach to bring our staff closer together. The Golden Star award is a small, 38-cent golden star that is issued to anyone who goes above and beyond to help in any aspect (e.g., developing curriculum content, etc.). Teachers nominate other teachers, and no teacher is ever turned away. Nominees wear this star to display their dedication to and support of the school. Although the awards were simple golden stars, staff members seemed to wear them with great pride, because they felt a feeling of satisfaction and accomplishment. By the end of the year, approximately 30 out of 80 teachers had received golden stars. Before long, the morale and motivation of the school staff had increased significantly.

In fact, during our last end-of-the-year staff meeting, the faculty presented me with an award—a golden star. But this was not the same 38-cent star I had given to them. It was a colossal star that is not only too large to wear, but takes up an entire wall in my home. I realized early on that making the most out of golden opportunities through acts of appreciation, no matter how simplistic, no matter how small, can make a colossal difference for principals, staff, and students.

SNAPSHOTS

People Are Always First

Susan G. Curtis
Franklin, Tennessee

The most important issue involved in the principalship or any leadership role is the way one treats people. People are always the most important part of the picture regardless of what one is trying to accomplish. People are number one. Students, faculty, parents, and community members must be considered over plans, programs, assessments, or issues. When people feel valued and respected, everything else falls into place. Best practices evolve as everyone does his or her part to enhance the effectiveness of the organization. People are allowed to give their input without fear of reprisal. People are complimented for the work they perform. People are recognized for their accomplishments and daily efforts. A culture of caring develops in the building as the school community works together to reach its ultimate potential.

Treat Others as You Want to Be Treated

Andy Adams
Alva, Missouri

Treat everyone in the building as you would want to be treated. I treated teachers, students, and parents as equals in dealing with the problems that we had. By doing this, the value of their opinions was shown. Then, when I incorporated several suggestions into discipline or building-level plans, they realized that I was truly in education for the gain and benefit of their child, and not for myself.

Shaping Culture to Turn a School Around

Andy Adams
Ava, Missouri

Without a doubt, I believe that shaping the campus culture is the most important thing to do to turn a school around and make it successful. Here are some things we have done at our school that have worked for us:

- When the kids would do something special, I filled a rolling trashcan with a fresh liner and popped enough popcorn to feed all 475 students. I delivered it to the classrooms and then hand filled individual popcorn bags. The kids loved it!
- We fill the building with quotes from famous people—"Never, never, never give up" (Winston Churchill). We have put these signs throughout the building and are quick to point to them for the encouragement of students.
- As principal, I know each individual in the building and make it a point to be in the hallway between classes. I am hands on, and the boys soon realized that little "scuffles" in the hallway with Mr. Adams would be fun and watched by all.

The building I inherited was in terrible shape. The first year I was there, I got more than 20 discipline referrals a day and was extremely discouraged. I then adopted the "long-term discipline" philosophy. I spent time with the students and learned the reasons for their behavior. I talked with them and did not just discipline them for the offense. In this way, self-discipline was instilled into the students, and they began to realize that they were responsible for their own actions. After seven years in the same building, I seldom had more than two discipline slips on any given day. By being at ease and making my staff and students feel at ease, we completely turned the building around.

Re-Establishing Campus Culture

Marla S. Brady
Boca Raton, Florida

We are learning a lot about re-establishing campus culture. During the past year, we enlarged our school by adding a class at every grade level and adding a high school. In all, we added 200 new students and 22 new faculty members. We have had to teach and model the culture to new students and new faculty. At the recent No Child Left Behind Blue Ribbon School conference, I heard another school talking about their similar experience. They said it took three years for them to regain the previous culture. It was good to hear that we were not alone in experiencing that phenomenon.

February Fun

Stan Beiner
Atlanta, Georgia

Every February, staff morale begins to decline. February is one month too many of blah weather. Contracts and placements are looming. Summer is far away. Having instituted this in my previous school in Kansas with much success, I made February a month in which we focus on keeping our teachers happy. Activities have included Jeans Fridays, a masseuse on hand for 10-minute massages, an ice cream party during lunch scooped by the administrators (they love calling us soda jerks—why?), soup of the week (a special soup cooked just for staff), a raffle, and so forth. The staff have really appreciated the attention, and the program brings lots of smiles to the teachers.

Co-Curricular Programs Shape Campus Culture

Stewart Carey
Westfield, New Jersey

Roosevelt School is unique in terms of the co-curricular programs offered to students. Our extremely active student council has received the Honor School Award from the New Jersey Association of Student Councils for the past six years. In addition, our student council donates approximately $20,000 per year to the New Jersey Association of Student Council's state charity. Our student council has been recognized as one of the best in the state.

We have an equally active peer leadership program that has also been recognized by the state for its outreach to students. More than 80 eighth graders are currently involved in our peer leadership program. They conduct learning activities for our sixth and seventh graders on character education, bully-proofing, and socialization.

In addition, we have more than 30 clubs and activities in which our students can be involved. The Reptile Club, a very active Junior Model United Nations Program, a literary magazine, a yearbook, a fall drama and school musical, a jazz band, an orchestra, and a premier choral group are some of the numerous offerings to students before and after school.

Roosevelt School has an active service program in which students support worthwhile community activities and reach out to those less fortunate. The Girls Learn International Club, the Blanket Drive for Appalachia, support for Westfield's September 11th Memorial, and brown-bag lunches for the homeless are among these services.

Summary

Shaping the Campus Culture Research: Develop and communicate a clear vision, understand the culture of the school, understand the change process, emphasize student learning, have high expectations, and support innovation.

**Best Practices for Shaping Campus Culture
From Award-Winning Secondary School Principals**

- Build trust
- Emphasize improvement for all
- Expect great things of everyone on campus
- Support new ideas
- Emphasize successes
- Meet the needs of all students
- Involve students
- Foster a positive environment
- Build positive relationships
- Commit to a shared purpose
- Treat everyone with respect
- Know your faculty and your students
- Know your school

SHAPING CAMPUS CULTURE REFLECTION

1. How would I characterize the culture on our school campus?

2. What do I do well on our campus to shape and maintain a positive campus culture?

3. What do I need to do to improve our campus culture?

4. What groups do I communicate with for greater community involvement in shaping and maintaining our campus culture?

5. Which ideas in this chapter do I especially like?

6. How can we implement these ideas in our school?

7. How might they need to be revised to be most effective at our school?

ADDITIONAL RESOURCES

No Child Left Behind Blue Ribbon School Conference
http://www.blueribbonschools.com

Texas Essential Knowledge and Skills
http://www.tea.state.tx.us

REFERENCES

benShea, N. (2003). *Inspire, enlighten, and motivate.* Thousand Oaks, CA: Corwin Press.

Blaydes, J. (2003). *The educator's book of quotes.* Thousand Oaks, CA: Corwin Press.

Covey, S. (1989). *The 7 habits of highly effective people: Powerful lessons in personal change.* New York: Simon & Schuster.

Cozemius, A., & O'Neill, J. (2002). *Handbook for smart school teams.* Madison, WI: National Education Service.

Deal, T. E., & Peterson, K. E. (1999). *Shaping school culture: The heart of leadership.* San Francisco: Jossey-Bass.

DuFour, R., & Eaker, R. (1998). *Professional learning communities at work: Best practices for enhancing student achievement.* Bloomington, IN: National Educational Service.

Fullan, M. (1999). *Change forces: The sequel.* Philadelphia: Falmer Press.

Jackson, A. W., & Davis, G. A. (2000). *Turning points 2000: Educating adolescents in the 21st century.* New York: Teachers College Press.

Matthews, L. J., & Crow, G. (2003). *Being and becoming a principal.* Boston: Pearson Education.

Newmann, F. M., & Associates. (1996). *Authentic achievement: Restructuring schools for intellectual quality.* San Francisco: Jossey-Bass.

Pang, V. (2005). *Multicultural education: A caring-centered, reflective approach* (2nd ed.). Boston: McGraw-Hill.

Payne, R. (1996). *A framework for poverty.* Highlands, TX: Aha! Process.

Winfrey, O. (2004, December). This month's mission. *O Magazine,* 28.

CHAPTER THREE

Communicating for Collaboration

A belief that every person brings an offering to a group requires us to include as many people as possible.

—*Max DePree (1989, p. 65)*

Good communication liberates us to do our jobs better. . . . Leaders can use communication to free the people they lead.

—*Max DePree (1989, p. 107)*

A collaborative culture builds leadership throughout every level of the school community as faculty, students, and the larger community work together to become colearners and coteachers. Including different aspects of the school family in decision making, required in some states as site-based management or site-based decision making, is another important role for the principal. This culture of reciprocity fosters purposeful learning that extends from the school campus into the larger community (Lambert, 2003). In fact, for principals to succeed in the 21st century, the school must count on community members for many kinds of support: resources, volunteers, discipline, ideas, input, advice, advocacy, energy, money, and more (Ramsey, 2005).

Although there are many ways for the community and the school to partner together in collaboration, they all begin with communication. As a best practice, open communication has been identified as one of the top five traits that effective schools have in common (Verdugo & Schneider, 1999).

Fullan and Hargreaves (2003) referred to communication as "positive politics." Senator Hillary Clinton, when commenting that the principal was the most important person in the school, added, "You have to be a politician and I'm sorry for that, but you do" (as cited in Blaydes, 2003, p. 144). Still, while maneuvering the sometimes emotional landscapes of interest groups and other diverse opinions and experiences, when principals collaborate through shared leadership, they become "hero makers" (Barth, 2003).

Collaborative school cultures value team process skills because members spend much of their time working together. Maeroff's (1993) research indicates that this type of collaboration requires effective communicating, trust building, and appropriate decision-making processes. Many of the communication for collaboration ideas that follow emphasize these research-based strategies, yet often they overlap in their focus for faculty, students, parent, and the larger community. For ease of reading, I organized them into two sections: communicating with faculty and other educators and communicating with students, parents, and the community. When noting these best practices, award-winning principal Diane Baker likens the role of effective educational leader to that of a "balancing or juggling act," because you are directly responsible for everything that occurs on your campus. In this balancing act, Tommy Floyd emphasizes the importance of involving faculty in decision making, but also challenges readers to be consistent in communicating that kids come first.

A best practice for Brent Curtice is to focus on faculty strengths, rather than their weaknesses. Other award-winning principals emphasize ways to use faculty meeting times and note the importance of communicating with parents through newsletters and surveys. For example, Stan Beiner considers one of his best practices to be surveying parents and then following through on some of their suggestions. Stewart Carey notes that communication is continual.

COMMUNICATING FOR COLLABORATION WITH FACULTY AND OTHER EDUCATORS

Kids First!

Tommy Floyd
Somerset, Kentucky

Begin your role as principal as a supporter, a helper, and an enabler. You will need to build the role of being a positive force for children; faculty and staff will not follow your lead in clutch situations if they think you are not there for the kids first! Here are some guidelines that have helped me be effective:

- Many times your teachers will disagree with your aim—listen to them every time! Stay focused on why you are going *this* direction; keep going back to the big picture. Make decisions based on how they will impact your best teachers.
- Be fair more often than right—this is one of the most misunderstood concepts in administration to date.
- Manage by walking around—this is your easiest tool to get out of that office! Keep walk-through documents and anecdotal records. Use a personal digital assistant with a walk-through document on Excel software, and use a cradle to synchronize it with your desktop. When you have summative conferences with teachers, you will have an amazing summative tool of what you saw over time as you stopped by. Show this record to them. It contains hard data, which can be very revealing!
- Avoid being reactionary—there are always two sides to every story.
- Show leadership by coming up with ways to support your teachers. Be a buffer, a listener, and an encourager!
- Determine who your leaders are and use them. Politics is nothing more than influence. Unify and then move on issues for school improvement.
- There are three groups on every staff:
  - Those who will do anything asked with enthusiasm—go to them first!
  - Those who are undecided—work the hardest on them; they still can join.
  - Those who are negative first—after the other two groups unify, they will not want to be left out or behind.
- Steadfastness, patience, and subtlety can result in the exact same outcome as stroke- and heart attack–inducing fits. Stress what is best for kids, not easier for teachers!
- Class time belongs to the students, not the computer, phone, newspaper, or anything else. A circulating teacher is one with fewer discipline problems.
- Use department heads and family leaders as much as possible for core content coverage, writing help, budget approval, inventory

control, school improvement plans, and general communication and accountability.

- Make sure everyone knows your expectations with regard to core content, writing process, and duties through meetings and department head reminders.
- With regard to faculty meetings, their frequency, e-mail, and preparation for them—failing to plan is planning to fail! Be accurate, be punctual, and consider appropriateness.
- My rule for faculty meetings is that I talk; see me after.
- Use e-mail for everything possible that will save having teachers meet. After school, they are tired, more apt to forget, and so forth.
- Plan on taking as much of the load away from your staff that you and your assistants possibly can to let the teachers teach. However, every now and then, remind them that you do this.
- Make your staff aware of how kids learn differently.
- Demand a variety of assessments in each classroom.
- Make your staff aware of the socioeconomic impacts your students face.
- Demand that your staff place the same importance on relationships with kids as they do on the coverage of their materials.
- Give recognition in walk-throughs and formal observations if you see teachers caring for kids in their rooms.
- Make absolutely certain, when faced with a situation in which a staff member seems indifferent to the needs of a particular child, that you bring circumstances to his or her attention in a tactful way.
- Remind faculty often how important they are in the lives of their students.
- Include your staff in graduation ceremonies with colors; let the graduates walk past them as they approach the platform.
- Build an environment of caring in your school—make it a priority!

Building Staff Leadership for Collaboration

Brent Curtice
Paonia, Colorado

Instead of focusing on staff weaknesses, I identify their strengths, using them in areas that will maximize the benefits for the school and for the students. I have empowered several staff members to capitalize on their own talents and to participate in opportunities for personal growth, which in turn results in a higher level of ownership, accountability, and shared vision.

Starting at the top, the administrative team, composed of the junior high school dean of students, the counselor or assistant principal, the athletic and activities director, and myself, meets regularly to coordinate the agenda of the school. I not only expect each individual to handle his or her area, but we also help each other problem solve, resulting in better decision making.

A staff leadership team, consisting of some of our trusted master teachers, focuses on curriculum direction and development, helps implement effective instruction, identifies testing and assessment tools, and mentors new teachers. A crisis team meets weekly to identify students at risk and to seek potential paths of assistance.

Just as relationships are vital with students for them to succeed, strong relationships with my staff members have fostered the belief that we are all responsible for both the instruction in and the daily operation of our school. Ultimately, "the buck stops here," which makes me accountable for everything that each committee endeavors to do. Again, I am a firm believer in group ownership and buy-in by all who have a responsibility for helping to deliver the product—the best education we can provide.

Sharing Our Successes

Dan Stepenosky
Beverly Hills, California

Beverly Hills High School (BHHS) continually shares information about our school through our Web site, through telephone and e-mail responses to inquiries from schools worldwide, and through administrative and staff contacts with other schools. On a national level, BHHS has a special relationship and maintains frequent e-mail communication with Council Rock High School in Pennsylvania, Columbine High School in Colorado, and Thurston High School in Oregon. Along with the director of guidance, we regularly visit other schools both inside and outside the district to share information about programs, innovations, success stories, and opportunities.

A significant component of our diversity program is visiting and hosting counselors, administrators, and teachers from Los Angeles Unified School District schools to discuss effective strategies and opportunities at

BHHS. The site leadership team is currently working on plans to produce a DVD that will showcase the school's exemplary programs and achievements. In addition, I am a member of a principal's consortium with principal members from 12 other local high schools that meets every two months to share information, assessment data, instructional strategies, and curriculum innovations. This consortium also hosts other educators, college admission officers, and local officials for roundtable discussions. Our assistant principals are beginning to formulate a similar consortium with counterparts from local secondary schools, with the goal of sharing information, providing resources, and creating a support network.

I am also part of an educational leadership cohort program at the University of California, Los Angeles, composed of 250 members from a variety of careers, including secondary school administrators, community college administrators, and private corporations. Members share information on a variety of educational issues including but not limited to school safety, equity issues in education, effective instructional strategies, legal issues, financial issues, and leadership techniques. BHHS is in the final planning stages of a $20-million science building that will house a large multipurpose room and a stadium-style theater with a large connecting courtyard. The design will provide a flexible space conducive to collaboration. Plans are to host events that will facilitate the sharing of information, including advanced placement and Academic Decathlon conferences, training sessions, community meetings, and orientation sessions.

Commit to Collaboration

Stewart Carey
Westfield, New Jersey

Our staff is committed to collaboration and teamwork. Effective instructional practices, ideas on differentiated instruction, sharing of interdisciplinary ideas, and general support for each other is the norm. We willingly share our ideas and gain ideas from other middle schools and other educational professionals. We have had numerous visits from other schools to look at our world languages program, our team teaching arrangement, our guidance program, and our differentiated instructional techniques. Cocurricular programs have been shared at state conferences held by the New Jersey Association of Student Councils and the National Association of Student Councils.

Our staff at Roosevelt School also shares our success with other schools by presenting at the New Jersey Principals & Supervisors Association and developing networks with other middle schools (which we have already started to do) to share ideas and concerns in areas ranging from special education to gifted and talented education programs. We continue to invite other professionals to Roosevelt School to view the program and dialogue with our professional staff. Developing a wider middle school network to share ideas and educational programs unique to middle schools is definitely a goal of our faculty and staff.

A Commitment to the Team

Marla McGhee
Austin, Texas

I had the joy and privilege of working with terrific assistant principals. We made a point of meeting face to face at the beginning of each week and would accomplish much as we took the opportunity to talk with one another and compare notes on our work. We would regularly review the calendar to help remind us of what was ahead. Likewise, we made decisions about who would attend special education staffing meetings and admission, review, and dismissal meetings as well as extracurricular events. As for our supervisory duties, we reviewed the classrooms and departments we had visited recently and reported on feedback we were providing for faculty and staff about various issues. If someone had questions or concerns about individuals, we could express them in this forum. Of course, we also shared successes here. Last and most important, this standing meeting gave us an opportunity to purposefully and meaningfully discuss the needs and progress of our students.

Role Modeling Effective Communication

Kathleen Haworth
North Hollywood, California

A principal is a school's role model for effective communication, both oral and written. It is important to maximize parent meetings, faculty meetings, and school newsletters as places to share the school's vision statement. As principals, we have to be sure we "know our audience" or, in other words, be very aware of the school culture. Middle- and upper-grade schools are unique cultures. Cultivating a sensitivity to and consideration of all stakeholders—parents, teachers, students, the community, and board members—is essential.

So many issues need to be considered when determining a school's vision and understanding its climate. Above all, you have to be realistic and know that there will be times of setback. The key is to allow your community to learn from each set of new challenges and to turn them into opportunities for learning and change. What may have been successful in one setting might not necessarily work in another.

Evaluating the players allows principals to determine the course of action and the possible solutions when dealing with the issues at hand. Information gathering is the best resource as the school's key leader introduces the vision to the community. An effective vision plan for a school will succeed if everyone feels that they have been heard and their input has been considered. Taking the time to engage the community will allow community members to buy into the plan.

Communication is again the key for success even in the intimacy of a one-to-one meeting with faculty, students, or parents. Timing and articulating the vision plan has to be well thought out in the same way that classroom curriculum has a scope and sequence.

Realizing Potential

Brent Curtice
Paonia, Colorado

The most important challenge I have had to face in the past five years has been the task of merging two levels of staff and schools into one unified system. Because each building brings with it a different set of philosophies, needs, strengths, and goals, my challenge has been to identify concerns, provide support and encouragement, and maintain the focus needed to attain our goals and shared vision.

Identifying concerns has been an ongoing process, as both the community and the staff were very vocal about perceived problems. Listening to and addressing those concerns publicly has been key. Combining the middle school and the high school accountability committees, along with using any and every public forum to advance our vision, I have been able to shift the focus of concerns to opportunities, possibilities, and partnerships. "How are we going to provide the best opportunities for students?" and "What is the best way of accomplishing our goals?" have been my focus.

Again, relationship building is vital. We spent days as a combined staff defining who we are and what is important to us. We have established high expectations for our students and staff; developed goals, strategic plans, and a realistic timetable; and then shared our vision with students and the community.

The results of these actions have created a more unified vision and direction among not only the staff and students, but also the community. The challenge continues, but our school community is about realizing potential rather than focusing on problems.

Listen and Be Safe

Diane Baker
Tularosa, New Mexico

First, I think that being an effective educational leader is a balancing or juggling act—you are handling at least 3 hot balls while juggling at least 10 more that are up in the air—because the educational leader is directly responsible for everything you have listed as topics for best practices, plus you are dealing with people, which means relationships.

The foundation of everything that an effective leader does is communication and collaboration, and most of what the leader does is listen and then figure out through collaboration what needs to be done. You listen to parents, to students, to teachers, to other staff members, to administrators over you—they all have concerns or issues, and usually, they want you to fix them. It is vital for the educational leader not to take on the burden of fixing as the sole responsible person, but to form collaborative teams. Sometimes I use a faculty meeting, breaking the teachers into teams and giving them the problem or issue to be addressed. I ask them to brainstorm and come up with one or two ideas. I give them two to five minutes and then ask for each team to share its ideas. From these ideas, I get a consensus for one or two ideas that we will implement. Then I follow up at the next faculty meeting to see how the ideas are working and what adjustments are needed. If I am listening to parents or students, I ask them what ideas they have to make the situation better. I use communication skills that empower people and make them part of the solution.

Every student, parent, and staff member needs to feel that his or her school is a safe place to be. After all, students and staff are spending the majority of their waking time at school. I start by charging every person with the responsibility of helping to maintain a safe environment. I do staff inservice training and beginning-of-school student orientations with PowerPoint presentations. Teachers must address issues as they occur. Students must report concerns, threats, bullying, and so forth to their teacher, counselor, or myself. We take every offense seriously and deal with each appropriately.

We have a weekly 35-minute period called Right Choices, which we use to educate the students on these issues. We have a block of time daily during the first week of school when teachers and students review and discuss the student handbook. Students are required to complete a study guide for the handbook. I make students responsible for their choices and actions. I make a daily announcement with the thought for the day on making right choices. When I am dealing with students and their discipline, I help them see that they make a bad choice when they react in a way that results in an office referral. We develop strategies to help them cope with situations so they can make better choices.

Communicating a Collective Vision

Eric Grantz
Bayside, California

Over the past three years, as an all-charter district, Jacoby Creek School has achieved a number of significant goals that have led to greater community involvement, diverse program offerings, facility improvements, and student achievement. This process began by engaging our entire school community in a yearlong process of developing a collective vision and strategic action plan. Today, this action plan successfully and very positively drives budget, program, facility, and curriculum decisions.

Another major key to our success is our faculty's commitment to ongoing and meaningful dialogue. Jacoby Creek staff meet three times each month in grade-level meetings, staff information and exchange meetings, and faculty meetings to formally discuss a broad range of grade-level-specific and schoolwide issues. Central to these discussions is our vision for the next five years and our commitment to maintaining the integrity and quality of our existing programs. Grade-level meeting agendas are set by the principal with input from the grade-level lead teacher, and meetings are attended by teacher groups (K–3, 4–6, and 7–8). Staff information and exchange meetings are no-agenda meetings designed to facilitate discussion on a variety of topics, including best practices, recent workshops, concerns, upcoming events, and so forth. Faculty meeting agendas are set by the principal and attended by all staff.

Another best practice that I am particularly proud of is our annual "student study" meeting. Each September, I hire four roaming substitute teachers for two consecutive days to free up classroom teachers so that we can meet and discuss each child in every class. We do this through a meeting with current and former classroom teachers, the counselor, the reading specialist, the speech teacher, the resource teacher, the gifted and talented education teacher, and the principal. During these two days, every child in the school is discussed, and if additional support is needed, the child is assigned to the appropriate specialist at this meeting. In this way, children with special needs are identified and supported very early in the school year.

Communicating and Collaborating With the Superintendent

Tommy Floyd
Somerset, Kentucky

Effective principals remember that superintendents want to help students too. We know how important superintendent support is for us at the school-building level. Here are some guidelines in working with your superintendent:

- Sit down with your superintendent as early as possible, and begin to build a supportive relationship.
- You can be effective to help your students many times without involving the superintendent, however, you cannot maximize your effectiveness without your superintendent's support.
- Stand on your own two feet from the beginning, and never surprise the superintendent with unpleasant information.
- Learn how often the superintendent wants communication, then do it!
- Find ways to get the superintendent into the building to participate as well.
- Never allow a negative discussion with staff about the superintendent to occur in your presence.
- Never enter into a negative discussion about the superintendent with a board member, no matter what! Discuss this issue and get his or her guidance on all board member discussions.
- Find ways to positively interact with the superintendent at all times.
- Children come first, even before superintendents. It is okay to disagree; find a way to seek a win/win situation.
- Superintendents did not likely get to where they are now unless they have already walked where you are. Never forget they preceded you in battle. They know what the trench is like!

Teacher Advisory Board

Stan Beiner
Atlanta, Georgia

To foster communication and team building, I created a teacher advisory board when I first arrived. Each month, I meet with teachers from various departments and divisions. The agenda is composed of topics that the staff would like me to consider as well as projects and ideas for which I need a sounding board. The advisory board was initially open to all staff. After the first year, we formalized the number of people (8–10) on the committee. People rotate on and off yearly. The agenda is shared with the entire staff via e-mail. Minutes are also distributed to everyone. The teacher advisory board has been especially instrumental in guiding me in such areas as salary increases, benefits, student dress code, and professional development.

The Lizard Lowdown

Marla McGhee
Austin, Texas

Although it sounds like a simple and relatively benign issue, faculty and staff on this large campus expressed they did not feel well informed or abreast of events and happenings at the school. I brought with me a practice I had used at my previous campus of writing and publishing a weekly newsletter and events calendar. Using the master calendar and other sources of information, I crafted *The Lizard Lowdown* (our mascot was the Lizard—yes, it really was!). The first portion of the bulletin was literally a day-by-day listing of events, meetings, scheduled games (volleyball, football, basketball, etc.), and other critical issues in the lives of the campus, faculty, and students. The remainder of the *Lowdown* contained various announcements of all sorts, helping us to stay more aware of what was happening and what was on the horizon.

Because *The Lizard Lowdown* was before the advent of campuswide e-mail and network systems, it was quite revolutionary. I also used this medium as a way to build community, celebrate successes, and create a sense of connectedness. I would occasionally embed a note into the *Lowdown* offering a free lunch, or soda, or something special to the first person to come find me. This was fun for all of us and kept many reading the *Lowdown* each week.

Communicating for Collaboration
With Students, Parents, and the Larger Community

Communicating Assessment Data

Dan Stepenosky
Beverly Hills, California

The school staff communicates individual student test results and grades to families by mail, through guidance conferences, on secure Web sites, through e-mail, and through personal student notification. Our assistant superintendent explains aggregated and disaggregated Standardized Testing and Reporting (STAR) test results in a televised board of education meeting. These testing data are also printed in the local newspapers, reported on the district Web site and in the school accountability report card, and presented to parents at Parent Teacher Student Association and eighth-grade orientation meetings.

Itemized STAR and California High School Exit Exam (CAHSEE) test results are mailed home to parents and students. Special-education teachers review student grade reports, and as part of each year's individualized education plan meeting, examine goals, administer tests to measure growth, and discuss results with parents and students. California English Language Development Test, STAR, CAHSEE, and proficiency writing tests results are discussed at English Language (EL) Advisory Committee meetings. The EL coordinator personally reviews all grades and test results with parents and discusses individual EL student results and proficiency standards in one-on-one meetings with parents, including mandatory redesignation meetings.

Forms are available in Russian, Spanish, Hebrew, Farsi, and Korean, as well as English, and translators are provided whenever requested. All new-to-district EL families receive important school documents and redesignation criteria in their home languages. Teachers also communicate assessment data for all participants to parents through information posted to the Micro Grade Web site, parent phone calls or conferences, and materials sent home requiring a parent signature.

Continual Communication

Stewart Carey
Westfield, New Jersey

There is continual communication with our parents and the general community concerning the academic data and individual student performance at Roosevelt School. On receiving the state testing scores, the school mails individual student results directly to the parents. School results are shared with our community via electronic newsletter, reports to our Parent Teacher Student Organization (PTSO), and reports by the district testing coordinator to the board of education, and they are disseminated widely through local media. Our involved, educated, and committed parents are very much concerned about their own child's progress, as well as the status of the Westfield Public Schools. As a result, they are very aware of and carefully read all information sent to them by the school and by the district.

In addition, parents regularly meet with guidance counselors, individual teachers, and teams of teachers to discuss their child's academic progress. High school students volunteer to tutor Roosevelt Intermediate School students after school. In addition, our eighth-grade peer leaders offer academic assistance to elementary and middle school students. Collaboration of parents and the school community provides valuable support to all the students at Roosevelt School.

On a daily basis, the electronic newsletter informs parents about the academic success of and student performance at Roosevelt Intermediate School. In addition, parent orientation programs are held throughout the year. Roosevelt has extremely supportive parents and an active PTSO that hosts parent visitation days for Grades 6, 7, and 8. It is customary to have more than 70% of the parent population coming to participate in their child's educational program. At our annual back-to-school night, it is usual that 100% of our student population has a parent present to hear about our academic program. Throughout the year, parents are involved in our PTSO meetings, orientation programs, and parent-teacher conferences, as well as support our numerous cocurricular activities.

Broken Window Survey

Stan Beiner
Atlanta, Georgia

Based on the idea that a community's health has something to do with its appearance and image (the Rudolph Giuliani approach to cleaning up New York), we asked parents, teachers, and community leaders to tell us what they loved about the school and what drove them crazy. We received more than 200 responses to the survey and broke the issues down. There are four planned Broken Window follow-up letters to give people updates on the changes being made as a result. We wanted to clearly communicate that we care about what people think. Thus far, we have taken down an annoying sign on the driveway, changed the cafeteria menu, and hired a math specialist. Next we plan to address carpool and parking issues (see Figure 3.1).

Student Academic Achievement Plan

Dana Trevethan
Turlock, California

Three years ago, in an effort to keep up and abide by our state's No Child Left Behind mandates, we created an evaluation tool to monitor students' progress on state and standardized assessments and grade-level mastery in EL arts and mathematics. The Student Academic Achievement Plan document has supported our counseling staff's desire and intent to provide our underperforming students and their parents with extensive academic counseling while connecting the data to both short- and long-term goal setting. We created the form to assist in the analysis of our students' STAR and CAHSEE results while working to guide them in the direction of onsite remediation and intervention opportunities. By closely monitoring our low-performing students' successes and lack thereof quarterly, our students and parents are now taking more advantage of our tutorials and special programs, which allow students to improve their reading and math skills as they work to achieve grade-level goals. In addition, our

Figure 3.1   Sample Letter

THE EPSTEIN SCHOOL
Solomon Schechter School of Atlanta

April 18, 2005

To: Epstein Family

I want to again thank everyone who participated in the Broken Window survey that was conducted in February. We had a great response. At this point, we have categorized the comments and are beginning to follow through on what was shared.

This is the first in a series of letters that I am sending to communicate on topics related to the survey.

I have heard two things which I would like to address:

Anonymity—Although some of you do not believe it, the fact is that your comments are truly anonymous. This is actually helpful to us because we don't look at the results and explain away remarks because of who made them.

Usefulness—Many of you thanked us for the opportunity to "vent." I have also heard from some that they did not respond because it was felt that we would not do anything with the survey. If you come to learn anything about our administration, it will be that your comments and ideas do matter and we do care.

How they stacked up—Here is the breakdown of responses (many shared multiple ideas, which is why the total may exceed 100%):

What Bothers You?

Carpool	17%
Program Questions and Issues	15%
Public Relations	9%
Administrative Issues	8%
Food	8%
Behavior Issues	7%
Dress Code	7%
Staff-Related Issues	7%
Parking	5%
Volunteerism Opportunities	5%
Facilities	4%
Tuition	3%
Miscellaneous	5%

What Do You Love About the School?

Caring Community	80%
Teachers/Administration/Environment	35%
Education	46%
Education—General	22%
Integration/Bilingual	8%
Judaics/Values	14%
Miscellaneous	2%

(Continued)

Figure 3.1 (Continued)

Open to Change and Being Cutting Edge	11%
Reception Area	6%
The Kids!	6%
Miscellaneous (Food, Communications, etc.)	4%

Action Item #1—Lunch: Linked, you will find a survey on our lunch menu. The kitchen staff, business office, and health committee want your feedback. You expressed your feelings and now it is time to learn more. Again, the survey is anonymous. SHARE YOUR THOUGHTS.

Click: http://snipurl.com/lunchsurvey   *The survey will be up through May 3.*

Action Item #2—Cartoon Sign: Some people commented on the cartoon sign on the fence that expresses loving one's neighbor. It looks cutesy, and most people from the outside don't read Hebrew. It is coming down. We'll use it elsewhere.

MORE TO COME—REMEMBER, YOUR VOICE DOES COUNT

B'Shalom,

Stan Beiner
Head of School

THE EPSTEIN SCHOOL
Two languages One community
שתי שפות קהילה אחת

staff, students, and parents are now better equipped and more eager to discuss the disaggregated data using common terminology that is used on our Student Academic Achievement Plan instrument (see Figure 3.2).

Outside Advisory Committees

Stan Beiner
Atlanta, Georgia

When I first came to the Epstein School, I asked for the establishment of a small group of advisors, not necessarily from the school. The advisory

Figure 3.2 Student Academic Achievement Plan (SAAP)

STUDENT ACADEMIC ACHIEVEMENT PLAN (SAAP)

Student: _____ ID: _____ Counselor: _____ Grade [ ]

Grade 9 (8th Grade Scores)	Grade 10 (9th Grade Scores)	Grade 11 (10th Grade Scores)	Grade 12 (11th Grade Scores)
California Standards Test	California Standards Test	California Standards Test	California Standards Test
ELA: FBB [ ] BB [ ]	**ELA:** FBB [ ] BB [ ]	**ELA:** FBB [ ] BB [ ]	**ELA:** FBB [ ] BB [ ]
Areas in Need of Improvement:	Areas in Need of Improvement:	Areas in Need of Improvement:	Areas in Need of Improvement:
Word Analysis Vocab. _____	Word Analysis Vocab. _____	Word Analysis Vocab. _____	Word Analysis Vocab. _____
Reading Comprehension _____	Reading Comprehension _____	Reading Comprehension _____	Reading Comprehension _____
Literary Response _____	Literary Response _____	Literary Response _____	Literary Response _____
Written Conventions _____	Written Conventions _____	Written Conventions _____	Written Conventions _____
Writing Strategies _____	Writing Strategies _____	Writing Strategies _____	Writing Strategies _____
MATH: FBB [ ] BB [ ]	**MATH:** FBB [ ] BB [ ]	**MATH:** FBB [ ] BB [ ]	**MATH:** FBB [ ] BB [ ]
Area of Assessment:	Area of Assessment:	Area of Assessment:	Area of Assessment:
_____	_____	_____	_____
Standards Masters - 75% needed to participate in Summer School. [ ]	*Standards Masters - 75% needed to participate in Summer School.* [ ]	*Standards Masters - 75% needed to participate in Summer School.*	
Goals: (Advanced, Proficient, Basic)	Goals: (Advanced, Proficient, Basic)	Goals: (Advanced, Proficient, Basic)	Goals: (Advanced, Proficient, Basic)
ELA: Range _____	ELA: Range _____	ELA: Range _____	**Passed Proficiency Exam:**
Math: Range _____	Math: Range _____	Math: Range _____	ELA [ ] Math [ ]
Passed CAHSEE: ELA [ ] Math [ ]	Passed CAHSEE: ELA [ ] Math [ ]	Passed CAHSEE: ELA [ ] Math [ ]	Passed CAHSEE: ELA [ ] Math [ ]
Recommended Interventions:	Recommended Interventions:	Recommended Interventions:	Recommended Interventions:
Tutoring (EL/Remedial/CAHSEE) _____	Tutoring (EL/Remedial/CAHSEE) _____	Tutoring (EL/Remedial/CAHSEE) _____	Tutoring (EL/Remedial/CAHSEE) _____
Home Reading 1/2 hr. _____	Home Reading 1/2 hr. _____	Home Reading 1/2 hr. _____	Home Reading 1/2 hr. _____
Parents Check Homework _____	Parents Check Homework _____	Parents Check Homework _____	Parents Check Homework _____
Homework _____	Homework _____	Homework _____	Homework _____
Weekly Report _____	Weekly Report _____	Weekly Report _____	Weekly Report _____
Summer School _____	Summer School _____	Summer School _____	Remediation Course _____
Remediation Course _____	Remediation Course _____	Remediation Course _____	Concurrent Adult School _____
		Concurrent Adult School _____	
Student Signature _____ Date _____	Student Signature _____ Date _____	Student Signature _____ Date _____	Student Signature _____ Date _____

members included the director of a nonprofit agency (and the parent of a former student), two very involved and influential community leaders (one parent and one parent of a former student), and a past president of the school. The purpose was to help me with the image of the school in the community and to assist me in navigating the politics that a newcomer will not be aware of. Three years into the job, the advisory group still meets with me, although the frequency has diminished.

The Tuesday Sheet

Lyman Goding
Plymouth, Massachusetts

Each Tuesday, every family can expect information from all teachers about the calendar, goals, and tips for home support and home conversation starters. Rather than staff doing notes or newsletters on different days, they are all done on the same day from everyone so that families know to expect guaranteed information on Tuesday. For example, the Tuesday Sheet on March 9, 2004, included information from Mr. Urann's math class about a test on inequalities and equations on Thursday. Mrs. Hartley in English shared that students would complete persuasive essays and noted that daily writing in class would be followed up with nightly revisions. Mrs. Jitiam in reading class wrote about the continuing newspaper unit. Mrs. Marconi noted that in geography class, students were finishing study of East Asia and would be taking an open-note test on Wednesday. Mrs. Lavin included information about a science unit on human body systems.

In a very short period of time, the Tuesday Sheet became part of the culture of the community and very much appreciated. No longer do parents get the blank stares when they ask, "How was school?" or "Do you have any homework?" or "What did you learn?" Now, much more concrete family conversations prompted by the Tuesday Sheet can be asked. The *Boston Globe* picked up on this idea and recognized it in their "Teaching Tips" column, and a number of other schools have adopted it.

Involving Parents

Heath Morrison
Waldorf, Maryland

I am very proud of the collaborative efforts established with our Thomas State High School community. Our PTSO and other parent organizations have fostered strong booster clubs in all areas including the fine arts and athletics. Our PTSO has monthly meetings and established agendas. We plan topics and seminars that are of interest to parents. For example, Advanced Placement Information Night, Scheduling Night, "Soon You're Going to Be a Senior," and high school transitioning have become fixtures in our yearly calendar. At the request of parents, we have established numerous programs, including weekend sessions, to help parents who have never gone to college prepare their children for the experience, and a progress report night, in which parents can come to the school and have a conference with their children's teachers before report cards are issued. We have also engaged in town meetings, at which we go directly into the community to address issues about the school, improvement plans, and our mission.

Connecting With the Community

Marla McGhee
Austin, Texas

When I arrived at C.D. Fulkes Middle School, one of the first things I heard from parents and community members was that they did not feel especially welcomed at school. I, too, noticed that the aesthetics of the entryway and layout of the front office did not look inviting to visitors. Faculty mailboxes were literally inside the front door of the office, and there was no place for visitors to sit. We immediately made changes, moving the faculty mailboxes to the workroom down the hall and replacing them with chairs, a sofa, tables, lamps, and artwork, creating an office reception area. We also had several attractive wooden benches made and placed them in the hallways outside the office. These physical changes, along with our renewed commitment to parents and community, seemed to make a positive difference.

Another way we reconnected with the broader community (and provided a safe and productive place for students after school) was to establish a series of late afternoon clubs and interest groups. Cooking, dance, small engine repair, and chess are just a few examples of the groups that were facilitated by parents, community, or faculty. Late buses provided transportation for students who wanted to attend.

Community Service Is a Winner

Lyman Goding
Plymouth, Massachusetts

We want students to make community service contributions to our school and community. Typically, we have nice things like food baskets, fundraising, cleaning, or painting. This year, we decided to participate in the Prudential Community Spirit program, which is open to both middle and high schools. We found a number of students doing community activities that we had not celebrated or did not even know about. Our participation prompted a large response and great community awareness that middle school students are old enough to do great things. As a result, I know that our school is perceived as much more than crazy or dangerous teens.

We ended up with a Prudential statewide "Distinguished Finalist" for a student's work in providing recreational supplies to the troops in Iraq who have little to do when not on duty, in the name of his cousin who was killed in Iraq. We also ended up with the National Middle School Winner (Lauren Stanford) out of 20,000 nominations, based on the student's raising about $400,000 for the Juvenile Diabetes Research Foundation (she has juvenile diabetes). In addition, we had a student who was diagnosed this year with polycystic kidney disease. She has decided to turn this into a community learning and service project based on having seen the experience of others here.

Real-Life Experiences Through Service Learning

Eric Grantz
Bayside, California

Another program at Jacoby Creek School that I believe helps us achieve high levels of student achievement is our service learning curriculum. Some of these community-based projects include restoring streams, raising and releasing salmon, growing food for our local zoo animals, making lap blankets for senior citizen rest homes, doing dune restoration and beach cleanups, fundraising for a leukemia foundation, collecting food for needy families during the holidays, doing get-out-the-vote campaigns, and so forth. These real-life experiences help students give back to the community while promoting a sense of stewardship and responsibility.

Community partnerships also promote valuable opportunities for our students. Our partnership with Humboldt State University currently includes (a) our classroom teachers working as mentors to university student teachers; (b) collaboratively developing and implementing grant-funded projects in science, math, and physical education that design model curricula and staff development opportunities for elementary educators; and (c) providing employment opportunities for university students who qualify under the federal work-study program as classroom tutors and instructors in our diverse afterschool enrichment classes.

Another unique partnership is done with a local cooperative grocery store, which provides a Harvest of the Month food tasting and nutrition education program for our primary students. Furthermore, we are the only school in California that has hosted a foreign exchange teacher through the American Field Service Program for the past two years, and our school community has benefited greatly by our sharing a teacher from China in 2003–2004 and currently sharing a foreign exchange teacher from Thailand. We also maintain a very active Jacoby Creek Children's Education Foundation, which provides $10,000 to $20,000 in program support to our school each year, and last, but certainly not least, we support a very enthusiastic parent volunteer program.

Summary

Communicating for Collaboration Research: Shared leadership, open communication, team building, and effective decision making that involves faculty, students, parents, and the larger community.

Best Practices for Communication for Collaboration From Award-Winning Secondary School Principals

- Be visible
- Listen to others
- Address concerns
- Become involved in the community
- Engage faculty and others in working as a team
- Encourage ongoing, meaningful dialogue
- Empower others
- Discuss data
- Share information
- Communicate expectations

COMMUNICATING FOR COLLABORATION REFLECTION

1. In what ways do I encourage collaboration at our school?

2. In what ways can I improve collaborative efforts at our school?

3. How do I communicate most effectively with faculty?

4. How do I communicate most effectively with students?

5. How do I communicate most effectively with parents and the larger community?

6. How can I communicate better with each group in the school community?

7. Which ideas in this chapter do I especially like?

8. How can I implement these ideas in my school?

9. How might they need to be revised to be successful?

Additional Resources

California High School Exit Exam
http://www.cde.ca.gov/ta

Gifted and Talented Education Teacher Golden Apple Teacher Education
http://www.goldenapple.org

Learning Styles
http://www.ncsu.edu/felder-public/Learning_Styles.html

Management by Walking Around
http://www.businesstown.com/people/communication-walking.asp

Personal Digital Assistant
http://www.pdastreet.com

Prudential Community Spirit Program
http://www.prudential.com/community/spirit

Standardized Testing and Reporting
http://star.cde.ca.gov

References

Barth, R. S. (2003). *Lessons learned.* Thousand Oaks, CA: Corwin Press.

Blaydes, J. (2003). *The educator's book of quotes.* Thousand Oaks, CA: Corwin Press.

DePree, M. (1989). *Leadership is an art.* New York: Dell.

Fullan, M., & Hargreaves, A. (2003). *What's worth fighting for in your school.* New York: Teachers College Press.

Lambert, L. (2003). *Leadership capacity for lasting school improvement.* Alexandria, VA: Association for Supervision and Curriculum Development.

Maeroff, G. I. (1993). *Team building for school change: Equipping teachers for new roles.* New York: Teachers College Press.

Ramsey, R. D. (2005). *What matters most for school leaders.* Thousand Oaks, CA: Corwin Press.

Verdugo, R., & Schneider, J. (1999). Quality schools, safe schools: A theoretical and empirical discussion. *Education & Urban Society, 31,* 286–308.

CHAPTER FOUR

Curriculum and Instruction

> Leaders look for a kind of transforming teaching and learning,
> where students are changed by what they learn, changed into
> deeper, richer human beings who want to use their learning to
> make the world a better place.
>
> —*Robert Starratt (2005, p. 65)*

As I write this, the headline in today's newspaper is large, black, and bold: "Feds Say 45 Area Schools Fail to Make the Grade" (2005). The article that followed this described the disappointment of area educators. Yet, as I read, I noticed that in every case, the school leaders interviewed acknowledged that they are already looking to more effective curriculum and instructional programs to meet the challenge. One leader described how his district is challenging special-education students and moving them back into regular classrooms. An assistant superintendent noted that the district has many recent immigrant students and will try a new reading program that is meant to accelerate learning for those students. This district will also provide students with handheld translators.

A major leadership role of principals is to manage the curriculum in ways that promote student learning. Geoff Southworth (2005) believes that this desire to enhance students' learning is "what makes school leadership distinctive and different from many other forms of leadership" (p. 75), and it is also at the heart of why many individuals become school leaders in the first place. There is no doubt that principal leadership influences what happens in the classroom, but because no principal can know everything there is to know about curriculum, much of this influence is largely indirect and done through modeling, monitoring, and dialogue (Southworth, 2005). After all, principals work with and through others—teachers, parents, and students. It is the principal's responsibility to stay informed of effective instructional practices and encourage and support the faculty to implement these strategies, then monitor and evaluate their effectiveness.

There are several ways that principals influence instruction, according to Hoy and Hoy (2003). These include

- encouraging academic excellence throughout the school,
- supporting continuous improvement among faculty,
- including teachers at the center of instructional improvement,
- providing resources and materials that support teachers in helping students,
- sharing best practices with faculty, and
- recognizing and celebrating academic excellence.

Award-winning principal Alan Mucerino, as instructional leader on his campus, points out that a best practice to ensure that effective instructional programs are in place is to structure the curriculum around the needs of students. Tom Hamilton shares the importance of involving students in authentic work. Other award-winning principals note the successes on their campuses of structuring curriculum through best practices that include standards-based curriculum, looping strategies, and the Creating Independence Through Student-Owned Strategies method. The curriculum involves everything that occurs at the school, even disciplinary procedures. Focusing on today's healthy lifestyles, Marilyn Svaluto shares a creative best practice for detention hall that incorporates walking and that is having a positive impact on the entire campus.

BUILD CURRICULA TO FIT STUDENT NEEDS

Allan Mucerino
Mission Viejo, California

As a former mathematics teacher and mathematics curriculum coordinator, I have held a strong belief in the idea that the curriculum should be built to fit the student, not the other way around. Many times, students struggle in school because the curriculum is not centered on their needs. As principal of La Paz Intermediate School, I believe that the curriculum should be kept adaptable and flexible at all times and responsive to ongoing evaluations.

Our school shares in the belief that our methods and materials should use a variety of resources and many learning modes to accommodate the individualities of the students. To that end, the organization is designed in such a way as to promote learning. Modeled after DuFour and Eaker's (1998) professional learning community, students are grouped flexibly and teachers are provided common planning time daily to meet. Meetings consist of analyzing and discussing student work and planning curriculum and instruction. Every classroom, then, is a safe learning environment in which students' needs drive curriculum and instructional practices on a more or less daily basis.

To strengthen and support the organization's commitment to learning, at La Paz Intermediate School, we partner with a variety of learning organizations and programs, including the University of Oregon's Center for Effective Collaboration and Practice to deliver effective behavior support. Effective behavior support is a schoolwide behavioral support program designed to prevent disruptive behavior by all students, including those who exhibit chronic behavior problems.

We also focus on communication, using a phone messaging program in conjunction with regular meetings, newsletters, and teacher Web sites with grades and assignments online, all designed to provide an effective and responsive system of outreach communications. Most families subscribe to our listserv and stay in close touch by receiving our daily bulletin electronically.

Like most successful schools, we believe the educational program should be the shared responsibility of the school, the home, and the student. Each staff member, parent, and student plays a significant role in the education program at La Paz. The organizational structure of La Paz is designed to ensure that students make a smooth transition from elementary school to high school. To facilitate smooth transitions, students are not isolated but instead are grouped heterogeneously with teachers, who have common planning time to meet regularly and work together to analyze student work, develop curricula, share instructional strategies, and monitor student progress.

Following the Gaining Early Awareness and Readiness for Undergraduate Programs model of creating a college-going culture, the school enjoys a unique relationship with a number of local university and community college sponsors. The focus of the relationships is to increase the number of students (particularly low-income and minority students) who are prepared to enter and succeed in postsecondary education.

Another nationally recognized program at La Paz with the same focus is Advancement Via Individual Determination. It was designed to increase schoolwide learning and performance by ensuring that the least-served students in the middle are given access to a rigorous curriculum that will allow them opportunity and success in completing a college path.

In addition, La Paz collaborates with a variety of schools and educators on several topics. It is also a host school for local teacher preparation programs, hosting as many as five student-teachers a year. We hold a number of annual and regional conferences that lend themselves to an open exchange of ideas and best practices. I continue to support these programs because they are extremely vital support systems for our children.

Student life extends well beyond the core-content classrooms. Students have numerous elective options in the fine and performing arts, technology, and communications. La Paz students are annually awarded for their performance in local (science fair), state (geography bee), national (MathCounts), and international (Knowledge Masters) competitions. Our school district maintains its own recreation department to provide all students with sports and other extracurricular activities before and after school and during lunch. Extended learning time provides an organized environment for students who seek extra help reaching decisions regarding their education.

We are committed to empowering and inspiring each student with the certainty of his or her individual importance and competence. We aim to provide opportunities and options by creating classroom environments that are rich and dynamic with role models and high expectations. We also consider every adult on campus a role model who must be personally responsible to model the very behaviors that we believe are most critical to the success of our students.

Closing the Achievement Gap

Tom Hamilton
Bardstown, Kentucky

Bardstown High School has a motto that focuses the decision-making process to a clear priority: "Do what is best for kids." In the education world, most decisions are made by adults, and many times, these decisions are made for their benefit rather than for the benefit of the students.

Bardstown High School is a public school in an increasingly growing community on the outskirts of a rather large metropolis. Gradually, the clientele has moved from a predominately white, suburban, upper middle-class student body to an enrollment that now includes 51% of students on a free and reduced-price lunch program and 25% who are minorities, mostly African American. In the new world of accountability, I knew we had to change the structure of our school to meet the needs of our changing environment.

As in most schools, our biggest concern was to address the achievement gap between our demographic groups, with two populations that have historically scored well below national standards on standardized tests, poor and African American children. The basic problem was to develop a schedule that maintained a rigorous curriculum but provided the flexibility to address the needs of students who were academically behind. Convincing the community to move from what we had always done to a schedule that was in the best interest of students was a tough sell.

Alternative School Calendar

Bardstown City Schools moved to an alternative calendar that allowed a two-week break between grading periods every nine weeks. Bardstown High School developed an intersession remedial program during one of those weeks to help students catch up without missing any regular class. In reality, some students (predominately from low-performing demographic groups) could get as many as 80 hours of additional instruction in the areas of reading, math, science, and social studies per year!

Engaging Students in Meaningful Work

Students are identified for remediation by grades and past history on standardized tests. Special policies have been implemented to engage students in meaningful work. After a few years of rather flat results, I implemented a policy that included a basic philosophical change. Instead of focusing on "make-up work" and worrying about what students cannot do, we began using exit criteria based on our school's core content to focus on doing better in the future. It produced immediate results.

Evidence

Here are the results: Since 1999, the number of students who were performing as novices (the lowest performance level on the state accountability test—the Commonwealth Accountability Testing System) has dropped from 28% to 13.9% in 2004. Overall performance has risen from an index of 67.7 in 1999 to 80.2 in 2004. Bardstown High School has met all its goals in both the state accountability and the federal No Child Left Behind goals. In 2004, Bardstown was designated a "rewards" school for meeting its goals in overall growth and reducing both the novice and dropout rate.

Even more exciting for those of us who work here, the percentages of low-performing demographic groups have risen steadily to virtually eliminate the achievement gap between white and African American students and greatly reduce the gap between the entire student body and poor children. Bardstown High School has produced similar results in all content areas and this year was recognized by the Kentucky Department of Education as a model school for closing the achievement gap.

STANDARDS-BASED CURRICULUM

Dan Stepenosky
Beverly Hills, California

Beverly Hills High School (BHHS) offers all students a broad, standards-based curriculum that provides various levels of complexity that engage all students with significant content.

The four-year English department curriculum is literature based and sequenced from developmental reading through advanced placement (AP). Vocabulary and standard written English conventions are integrated into the literature and studied as discrete units. A comprehensive writing curriculum includes mastery of the thesis paragraph essay in tenth grade, research papers in tenth and eleventh grades, and creative writing across all grade levels. Tenth and eleventh graders take a writing assessment placement test.

The mathematics program offers a full range of courses for students of varying ability levels. The college preparatory sequence offers two paths. Both begin with algebra. The liberal arts student continues with basic geometry, intermediate algebra/trigonometry, and either probability/statistics and finite math or functions, statistics, and trigonometry. Math and science students take geometry, advanced algebra/trigonometry, math analysis, and AP Calculus. Students from either path may take AP Statistics. Non-college-bound students take Math Workshop or Math A, and algebra, in a one- or two-year program.

In the science program, all students take one semester of health and a minimum of one year of life science, and one year of physical science from life science, biology, honors biology, physiology, physical science, chemistry, physics, AP Biology, AP Chemistry, AP Environmental Science, or AP Physics. Science classes are lab based and include numerous hands-on projects, such as Amgen recombinant DNA labs related to research on gene therapy, production of Factor 8, and DNA fingerprinting; circuitry labs; projectile motion labs; oxidation reduction; and acid-base titrations.

In the social science program, all students take world history, U.S. history, American government, and economics. A ninth-grade humanities class combines the study of world history and English and integrates literature with historical topics. AP European History is offered as a tenth-grade elective. Courses are provided for all levels and abilities, including developmental, English learners (EL), and AP. The developmental and EL curricula are parallel to that of regular classes.

Our extensive arts curriculum emphasizes technique, performance, appreciation, history, and professionalism. Performing arts courses include concert choir, minnesingers, madrigals, band, beginning instruments, symphony orchestra, music appreciation, piano workshop, introduction to theater arts, drama lab, screen acting, theater arts workshop, film/cinema, and technical theater. Visual arts course offerings include Art 1–2, contemporary crafts, drawing and painting, graphic design, AP Art History, life drawing, studio art, and AP Studio Art. Both the performing and visual arts students successfully participate in festivals, fairs, and competitions throughout the year.

Foreign language courses include seven levels of Spanish, five of French, and four of Hebrew, all with an organized system of instruction by levels. One year of foreign language is required, but in 2004, 46% of the student body enrolled in higher-level courses. In each of the languages, students learn to speak, read, write, and appreciate the culture of native speakers.

Technical arts courses provide a rich diversity of courses in media, journalism, architecture, creative woods, and photography, including residential and advanced architecture and commercial building design; beginning and advanced creative woods; beginning and advanced computer graphics; beginning, advanced, and broadcast journalism;

yearbook; beginning and advanced photography; and five media classes, including beginning, advanced, and field courses.

The special-education department enables all students to have access to the core curriculum, provides transitions into the adult community, and meets state and federal regulations that are consistent with the district mission statement. The subject areas addressed in the remedial program are U.S. history; government; economics; and ninth-, tenth-, and eleventh-grade English. To help students transition from the high school environment to the demands of adult life, transition is addressed in the individualized education plan at age 14, with an individual transition plan at age 16.

Physical education has a three-year requirement, and students progress from beginning to advanced skill levels to enhance health and fitness.

Most recently, the high school leadership team developed a three-year phased-in benchmark (common) assessment plan that will standardize course sequencing, content, and assessment techniques, and, using the benchmark data, colleagues will be able to work collaboratively on effective instructional strategies.

Supporting Standards-Based Programs

Diane Baker
Tularosa, New Mexico

Effective instructional programs involve many components. Their foundation must be based on the state's standards and benchmarks and an assessment of what each student has mastered. We use results of formal and informal testing and teacher input. I use a spreadsheet to list each student by grade level. I have columns for test results in reading and math and what reading or math program level the student is ready to start. I ask the teachers to provide input on a separate spreadsheet about each student's level—high, medium high, medium, or low skill level for reading and math. I have columns for this information on my master spreadsheet. This provides the information for scheduling and assigning classes.

I believe that instructional programs in reading and math must be implemented by skill level with high expectations for learning and mastery. Our rule of thumb is that 80% of the students must demonstrate

80% mastery for every skill or benchmark. For students not meeting the 80% rule, we develop an academic plan with them and parents. We do not use social promotion; the students must master the academic skills at their grade level to move forward.

Teachers are held accountable for teaching to mastery—this (as with everything else) is a process. Teachers have been used to "covering" materials, and it was up to the students to get them. Teachers are required to identify key concepts that students must know and be able to demonstrate by the end of school. Teachers randomly sample these key concepts weekly. This allows for a preview of skills to come and a review of skills taught. Students are not graded on the random sampling, but they chart the results individually, and the teacher charts each class. This allows students to compare how they are doing in the class and with other classes. As the year progresses, the dots on the run charts go up, indicating more correct responses. The technique is used for retention of the key concepts. We do not give students "permission to forget."

Teachers work on higher-order thinking skills as defined in Bloom's taxonomy. Thirty percent of the items on assessments must be analysis, synthesis, or evaluation. The other 70% of items can be from the three lower levels of Bloom's taxonomy (knowledge, comprehension, and application).

I became an administrator to support teachers. I believe that teachers have the most important and vital job in the whole world. I also believe teaching is the hardest job. Therefore, teachers need supportive principals and leaders. They need principals who have "been there and done that" and remember what it is like in the classroom. Supervision that supports teachers and the instructional program is vital. I have an open door—teachers come to me with concerns about students, curriculum, and so forth. We work together because we are a team with the same goal—to provide the best education possible to every student in our school. Teachers know that I am their coach, their mentor, their supporter—whatever they need, and not just professionally, but also personally. They are not just teachers, but mothers, fathers, husbands, wives, sons, and daughters. Often, personal needs must be met for the teacher to be able to fulfill his or her professional responsibilities. Classroom observations and visits are to support the teacher; therefore, immediate feedback is provided. I try to schedule observations just before the teacher's preparation period so that we can have that time for collaboration.

Students, society, and expectations placed on schools have changed drastically over the past several years. We are required to teach what families used to teach, we start kids younger (preschool programs) and keep them longer (we are responsible for postgraduation data collection and reporting), and we do before and afterschool programs—and all with limited resources. Teachers feel stressed; the more I can do to relieve the stress, the more teachers are able to focus on teaching and student learning.

At our school, we work on continuous improvement. Five years ago, our school participated in a state initiative called Strengthening Quality in Schools. The focus was to use Malcom Baldrige's (http://www .baldrige.com) quality criteria developed for improving businesses by looking at the systemic parts and how they function. Our staff has been trained (and new staff are also trained) in strengthening quality techniques for continuous improvement. We implement "plan-do-study-act" at all levels (student, classroom, and school). Decisions are based on data collected. We are continuously looking at what are we doing, how is it working, and what we need to be doing.

Continuous improvement is a process. It does not happen overnight, and it takes a lot of work to make changes. Everyone—teachers, students, custodians, secretaries, and food-service providers—must support the school's vision and mission. We use Jim Shipley's integrated systems solutions (e-mail jimshipley@mindspring.com for information) for continuous systems checks to evaluate how we are doing on the seven criteria: leadership, strategic planning, student focus, information and analysis, human resource focus, management of processes, and results. In 2003, we were recognized with a Pinon Award by Quality New Mexico.

CHALLENGING CURRICULA

Stewart Carey
Westfield, New Jersey

Roosevelt Intermediate School is a 45-minute commute from New York City in a suburban community with a rich cultural and historical heritage. A rigorous academic program in all curricular areas enables our students to perform extremely well on the Grade Eight Proficiency Assessment, a four-day test encompassing science, reading, writing, and mathematics. In sixth, seventh, and eighth grades, students are divided into two teams. Teachers on each team are responsible for the academic program in math, world languages, language arts, social studies, and science for approximately 130 students. This provides a home base for each student in a smaller unit. Each team has a leader and meets regularly to plan curriculum and plan for the individual needs of its students. The team provides a coordinated, interdisciplinary curriculum structure and meets the academic, social, and behavioral needs of the students.

The curricula at Roosevelt School are engaging, challenging, rigorous, student centered, and focused on differentiating instruction to meet the needs of all students. Each area of the curriculum is reviewed every five years and is based on the New Jersey core curriculum standards. A professional staff of certified teachers ensures Roosevelt Intermediate School has a challenging and rigorous program for middle school students.

The mathematics program is exceptional. All students in sixth grade take prealgebra. In seventh grade, a majority of our students are placed in Algebra 1. Over two years, well over 90% of our students complete a rigorous Algebra 1 program. Students who are not ready for the formal study of algebra are placed in an algebra preparation course.

The highly demanding language arts curriculum produces excellent student writers. All students write research papers and complete writing portfolios using the department computer lab. They are competent readers who analyze multiple genres of literature at each grade level.

The world languages program is unique. In sixth grade, all students select French or Spanish, which they take every day for their entire three years as a student at Roosevelt. Students who select Spanish build on their four previous years in elementary school studying Spanish. Our students are exposed to the conversational language and cultural study of these two areas for an extended period of time. The world languages program is rigorous, is exciting, and provides our students with the opportunity to have a solid foundation in French or Spanish by the end of their eighth-grade year. The staff continually upgrade the program and work collaboratively to enhance this experience for our students.

Our science program is taught by a group of dedicated teachers, all certified in science. The program provides for lab experience and is very student centered. The hands-on approach incorporates life, physical, and earth sciences in each of the three years that our students take science. The program is based on both national and state standards in science and is a spiral program of earth science, physical science, and life science at each grade level, allowing students to build and refine concepts as they progress through middle school. Technology is used in each science classroom to complete labs, do Internet research, create charts and graphs, and use CD-ROMs and simulation programs.

The Roosevelt School social studies curriculum has been newly redesigned based on state and national standards. This curriculum is student centered, and its focus is to help develop world citizens who have an understanding of history and can be contributing members of our democracy. Our sixth-grade program focuses on Eastern traditions, the seventh grade on Western traditions, and the eighth grade on early American history and the U.S. Constitution and our form of government. Debate, presentations, technology, and forming educated opinions, as well as ongoing research, are all part of our social studies curriculum.

In sixth and seventh grades, our students have music every day, and they have art for half a year. Students may select band, orchestra, or chorus as they enter sixth grade as part of their music program. Eighth grade offers a unique opportunity for our students to select from a number of art and music classes, as well as drama, for a full year of instruction. More than 80% of the students are involved in art and music on a regular basis. This represents the community's cultural heritage and emphasis on having students actively involved in the arts.

Technology is integrated into all of our curricular areas. A technology class in computers and the basics of technology is offered to sixth graders. In eighth grade, an elective program gives students the opportunity to select among a number of options that include journalism, drama, fine arts, woods, and advanced computer instruction, as well as orchestra, band, and chorus.

FRESHMAN INDUCTION AND LOOPING
IMPROVE PERFORMANCE

Kevin R. Fitzgerald
Camden, Delaware

Caesar Rodney High School (CR), founded in 1919 and named after the Delaware patriot Caesar Rodney, has always prided itself on providing a quality education for its students while at the same time serving as a focal point for community activities. Throughout its long history of serving the greater Camden-Wyoming, Delaware, communities, the school has seen the construction of a new high school in 1967 and a massive $32-million renovation that was completed in the spring of 2005. The school currently has more than 1,800 students enrolled.

CR has consistently maintained an emphasis on the basics in education. With the implementation of the Delaware State Testing Program and state standards, CR worked to capitalize on its philosophy of adhering to the basics and what it considered to be sound educational research as it worked to improve student performance. The consistency of leadership and program has enabled the high school to display overall growth in student achievement as a result. Three major changes were implemented to increase student achievement and foster a smaller learning environment. They were

- 2000–2002: Looping was instituted in English and math classes for Grades 9 and 10. This provided continuity in instruction for the students, allowed the teachers to concentrate on helping student achievement, and made for a smooth transition from middle school through the state testing program. The ninth- and tenth-grade academy was created.
- 2002–2003: Freshmen orientation day was created.
- 2003–2004: Eighth-grade orientation night combined with specific scheduling nights for three different middle schools and choice students allowed incoming freshmen to meet with school personnel (counselors, administrators, teachers) and become aware of opportunities for challenging courses. The school was named a superior school based on a rating by Delaware.

I believe that the changes that we have made have helped shape our school culture, enhanced our instruction, and greatly assisted us in meeting the No Child Left Behind targets.

Induction Programs

Seeking to work toward improving student performance, the staff participated in several indoctrination programs designed to get incoming freshmen acclimated to their new school and to the expectations the school staff has for all students. In February of each year, the school conducts an open house for prospective students. Students and their parents tour the facility and listen to presentations from members of each department, explaining the various course offerings and other programs available at CR. Students also meet student leaders in the cafeteria, where they get a preview of clubs, organizations, and athletic teams that students may join. All eighth-grade students in the district receive a book containing a selection of short stories to be read over the summer.

Then, during the first day of the regular school year, only freshmen report to school as they participate in a freshmen orientation day. They are assigned faculty mentors who review school policies, share valuable study hints, and discuss the summer reading. The English department provides further instruction during the course of the school year using the same texts. This orientation enables students to follow their class schedule, meet the teachers, and find their way around the school. Guest speakers inspire students with their motivational stories. The day concludes with students taking a practice PSAT, which has provided the school with helpful data and prepares students to take the PSAT. This practice and the offering of the PSAT at a later date for all freshmen and sophomores has led to an improvement in PSAT scores and enabled more students to take the tests. The testing has also facilitated the identification and encouragement of students who should be taking AP courses.

Pleased with the results of the freshmen orientation program, I proposed to the school board an additional day to be designated just for sophomores; also, the administration and staff are developing a program for the interests of students ready to build on the freshmen orientation and consider topics like the SAT, the Delaware State Test, career and vocational studies, and the college selection process.

Looping

Another practice that CR has followed to improve student achievement is the looping of teachers in English and math and, to a limited degree, looping in science and social studies. Students are assigned a teacher in ninth grade for English and math, and that same teacher goes with the student through tenth grade. The teacher and student become familiar with each other, teaching and learning styles mesh, and more individual attention is devoted to the problem areas of the student. With this added attention, performance improves over the two-year period. To further facilitate this arrangement, a ninth-grade academy was started with the freshmen English and math classes scheduled in the same wing and on the same floor of the building; sophomores were scheduled on the other level. This allows for the sharing of lesson plans and use of common vocabularies between the two disciplines. Again, these activities were planned to enhance student performance. The science classes are clustered nearby, as are the social studies offerings; thus, the academy students are with their peers much of the school day. This allows the students to feel like members of a smaller learning community rather than just being "a face in the crowd" of one of Delaware's largest high schools.

Looping Aids Accountability

Becke Cleaver
Winchester, Kentucky

I am principal at Conkwright Middle School, a traditional rural school with a magnet school-within-a-school for gifted and accelerated learners combined with a unique population. I would like to talk about our best practice. It has been five years in the making. We are looping schoolwide but in a very unique way: Each teaching team has all three grades from sixth through eighth. Students enter as sixth graders and are assigned to a teaching team and remain with the same teachers for all three years of middle school.

There are many positives as well as challenges in this approach. For example, it is more work for teachers, as they do three preparations a day. Each team has one teacher of language arts, math, science, social studies, and special-education collaboration. Also, each team has one double batch per grade, which provides a way to infuse total collaboration for special-needs students, and the special-education teachers get to stay with their students for all three years as well (see Figure 4.1).

Accountability rests with the teachers. If there are low scores for students in a subject, we do not look to all teachers in that subject, but instead to just one. Accountability for me is a huge issue, because I cannot afford to have a student with a marginal teacher for three years.

The biggest reason not to loop using this team approach was the issue of a behavior problem or a personality conflict between a teacher and a student, or between students. I have seen situations when teachers just have one grade each year, and often behavior problems were just tolerated, then passed on to next year's teacher to handle. Often, I would see the same behaviors in students recur each year. Sometimes teachers would collaborate to implement procedures to stop the behavior, but still the student would

Figure 4.1   Looping Pattern at Conkwright Middle School

Each team in the school has one double batch at each grade level. The magnet team, due to population, maintains two batches of each grade level. The teams with the double batches are where the special-needs population for that grade level is placed so that the special collaboration teacher on that team also has the advantage of having the same students on his or her caseload for the three years of middle school.

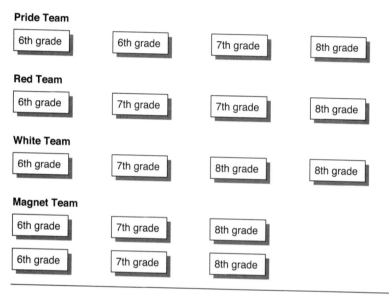

try it again the next year. But we have found the teaching teams work harder to find a solution to any behavior problems because they do not just pass students on to the next team the next year. They deal with it. They know that they are going to live with the child with problems, so they try to find a more workable, long-lasting solution.

Team looping is one less change in the changing lives of middle schoolers. It eliminates the start-up time at the beginning of the year, and teachers quickly move into the next year's curriculum as they wind up the year, so instructional time is increased. We also are seeing a trend of increasing the number of parent conferences called by the teaching teams in their efforts to seek long-lasting, positive solutions to student problems.

Before looping, our teaching teams had two planning periods while their students were in related arts classes. But now we have morning grade-level related arts classes (i.e., all sixth graders from all four teams come out of the academic looped team to go to related arts). This creates the need to have some of the teachers plan together. In the afternoon, the students come off the academic teams by team, which creates teamwide planning. We made sure that teachers during individual planning time were planning by subject. Now, for the first time, team collaboration by subject has increased considerably! This has also increased the support of the language arts teachers as they complete portfolios. The sharing of ideas is very good. Prior to this, I have never been able have a middle school schedule in which our subject teachers could get together and plan during the day.

Team Looping Shares Responsibility

Becke Cleaver
Winchester, Kentucky

At Conkwright Middle School, we do writing portfolios in the seventh grade. In the 10 years that I have been at Conkwright, with 8 of the years before we started to move into looping, I never kept a seventh-grade language arts teacher longer than 2 years, and often, a first-year teacher right out of college would be willing to take the seventh-grade language arts class just to get the job. I had to move two really good teachers out of the seventh-grade language arts position just to save them from the stress. Now, instead of one teacher being responsible for 170 portfolios, four language arts teachers share the load. In our old pattern, the teaching teams had one grade, which meant the language arts teacher on the seventh-grade team had all the writing portfolios to complete. Seventh graders complete the portfolio in middle school in Kentucky, so all 170 seventh graders were on one team.

Now, all four teams have sixth, seventh, and eighth graders. This means that four language arts teachers work with their seventh-grade groups to complete the portfolios. The portfolio is a year-long project, and it is very involved and very stressful. Now, with four teachers each doing a much smaller total of portfolios, it is not as stressful. Of course, we are keeping specific data. Last year was our first schoolwide year to use a team looping approach, and we already have our data about portfolios. We only had 7 novice-level portfolios in the entire school, compared with 48 the year before.

THE ROLE OF TECHNICAL ARTS

Dan Stepenosky
Beverly Hills, California

In keeping with our school mission and objectives, the technical arts department prepares students for higher education and employment, teaches critical problem-solving skills, and affords students the opportunity to explore areas of personal interest. Career awareness and employability skills are interwoven throughout the entire technical arts curriculum via cooperative learning, role playing, simulations of the workplace, and extensive use of product-oriented assignments. For example, in architecture, the student becomes the architect and designs and creates a model of a house for a particular client and lot. Using a state-of-the-art computer lab and software, students in computer graphics form companies that bid on projects and design and produce various products, including T-shirts, brochures, and posters. They also recently revamped the masthead for the school newspaper and are currently creating the graphics for Norman-Aid stations that will be stationed around campus to hold important school and community resource information for students.

Woods and photography classes tap students' creativity while honing their technical skills, enabling them to produce exceptional, award-winning end projects. Journalism students become the editor and staff writers of the school paper. The student-run TV station, KBEV, is aired on local cable. Students function as writers, producers, directors, video editors, engineers, camera operators, graphic designers, announcers, or reporters, depending on their interests and skill levels. A broadcast journalism class integrates both areas as journalism students write and deliver the news on KBEV. Math, reading, and writing are integral components of all technical arts classes.

Math skills are reinforced in calculating measurements, developing a budget, calculating amounts of wood, and producing scale drawings and models. Writing skills are developed in every course through assignments such as writing TV production scripts, news and yearbook articles, technical reports, architectural critiques, photographer reports, and captions for scripts and ads. Teachers emphasize the development of reading skills through texts, supplemental readings, articles, and written directions. The practical nature of all assignments requires critical thinking, analysis, evaluation, problem solving, and creativity. Technical arts students leave BHHS well prepared for college-level coursework and the workplace.

CRISS-CROSS PROFESSIONAL DEVELOPMENT

Evelyn Ennsmann
Villa Park, Illinois

At Willowbrook High School, we have a reading requirement that students must pass before they graduate. To help us achieve this important goal, we have incorporated Marzano, Pickering, and Pollock's (2001) book *Classroom Instruction That Works* with Project CRISS (Creating Independence through Student-owned Strategies), which we call CRISS-CROSS. This model engages students in effective behaviors for reading texts across the content areas. All of our English teachers have been CRISS trained, and they are training other staff. The reading teachers also share best practices and teach other strategies across the curriculum.

It is important that all of us share a common language and common strategies across all disciplines. The strategies that are emphasized include setting objectives and providing feedback, using cooperative learning, summarizing, note taking, using cues and questions, generating and testing hypotheses, advancing organizers, and identifying similarities and differences.

To make the best use of school time for professional development, our building leadership team (department chairs and building administration) and our teacher-leaders provide the CRISS-CROSS training to staff at our "Lunch and Learns." During these times, our teachers come in and work on the training while having lunch. These are held every two weeks. The Lunch and Learn settings are just one example of how we work together at Willowbrook High School—both district and building leadership—with our teacher-leaders to provide a climate of learning for all students.

Another way that we have provided for staff development is our late Monday start. Students come to school one hour later during this time. Teachers come at the regular time (7:45 a.m.) to have dialogue, share problems, and practice work in teams, and English teachers CRISS-CROSS train during this time. The students and teachers love this!

Emphasizing professional development and using school times with Lunch and Learns and late Monday starts have helped created a professional learning community. In addition, they have created a sense of oneness across disciplines.

DIFFERENT INSTRUCTIONAL METHODS IMPROVE LEARNING

Dan Stepenosky
Beverly Hills, California

At BHHS, teachers use many instructional methods to facilitate learning, including coaching, collaboration, field trips, instructional drills, homework, independent research projects, portfolios, service learning, career applications and connections, integrating interdisciplinary concepts, integrating lecture and discussion sessions, lab opportunities, sheltering strategies, and technology delivery systems. Understanding that not all students learn in exactly the same way, BHHS teachers also employ the simultaneous use of verbal, visual, auditory, and kinesthetic strategies if appropriate.

Career learning experiences include an Amgen lab in honors biology, water- and air-testing activities in environmental and AP Environmental Science, and building activities in physical science, all of which connect students to problem-solving skills. Applications to the physical and social sciences are explored in finite math, math analysis, and probability/statistics. Hi-Map units are used in finite math group projects. Student learning is also improved through creating end products: Journalism students are editors and staff writers of the school paper. Broadcast journalism (combining journalism and media) students produce weekly cable newscasts. Architecture students, using MicroStation 2D and 3D CAD and MicroStation Triforma, design and create houses for particular clients. Service learning projects illustrate the application of science to the real world. In one case, life science students studied the immune system, researched vaccines, and then raised more than $900 for the United Nations Children's Fund to help eradicate polio worldwide.

Technology applications, another integral tool in the learning process, include library technology; graphing calculators in math; films and audiotapes in foreign language; equipment for TV broadcasting, woodworking, photography, and architecture; a piano keyboarding lab in performing arts; word processing and research for essays, research papers, and projects in English, foreign language, and social studies; lab equipment for science; and computers for instructional delivery. Special-education students in fine arts, physical science, and life science use campus computers extensively. Fine arts students have taken virtual tours of many museums, used word processing to create biographical sketches of artists, and learned to download graphics for insertion into reports. Students in life science participate in the Global Learning and Observations to Benefit the Environment (GLOBE) Project, submitting weather data from BHHS via the Internet to the GLOBE Project Web site online. EL students also use technology to increase their learning through an expanded curriculum.

DIFFERENTIATED INSTRUCTION OPPORTUNITIES

Stewart Carey
Westfield, New Jersey

Teachers design lessons with a focus on what students should know, understand, and be able to do. Teachers are committed to following our curriculum and making sure that learning experiences are student centered, are directed toward goals and objectives, and provide for individual student assessment and learning. There is a focus on differentiated instruction, which provides teachers an opportunity to meet the needs of the variety of learners in their classrooms. Teachers regularly tier lessons for student ability and provide a variety of lessons for student interest.

In addition, our teachers make themselves available for extra help before and after school on a daily basis, as well as provide an array of enrichment activities for students. An example of this is the International Club, in which some of the top students in world languages provide an opportunity for a scavenger hunt for sixth and seventh graders with all directions and clues written in their targeted world language. This event takes months to plan and provides a true enrichment opportunity for students in the area of world languages.

A gifted and talented education program enables students to explore areas such as finance, inventions, and debate. The Teddy Roosevelt Scholar Program affords our top eighth graders the opportunity to be involved in a yearlong rigorous independent research project with a mentor-teacher. For the past six years, this program has challenged the most talented students.

Our special-education program provides support for our special education students. Each special-education teacher is assigned to a team to ensure that student individualized education plans are fully implemented. Supplemental classes provide support for students' regular academic classes.

In-class support in several subject areas, as well as the collaboration between regular education and special-education teachers, provide for the needs of our special-education population.

Our library/media center provides an opportunity for research, resources, reading materials, and additional instructional support in all subject areas. The technology in our library, computer labs, and classrooms enhances student research, reading, and writing abilities. Our library/media center specialist continually provides current and cutting-edge materials for staff and students.

ACADEMIC CELEBRATIONS

Lyman Goding
Plymouth, Massachusetts

At Plymouth Community Intermediate School (PCIS), we have several different academic celebrations and programs that contribute to more effective instruction. Here are some of them:

- "Homework Heroes" is a parent-sponsored activity that celebrates Grade 8 students who do 100% of their homework per term. High school students who were former homework heroes come back and share success stories and the value of doing homework as well as transition information.
- Students of the Month: About 30 students are honored every month for a variety of reasons—academic success, great gains, or community or school service. The program is taped by students and broadcast on local cable. Families are invited, and this program is run in the old honor society way: We do not tell the kids, but call their families in advance. The parent association has purchased a lobby display board and bumper stickers ("Proud Parent of a PCIS Student of the Month" or "Proud Grandparent of a PCIS Student of the Month"). This event is so well received and appreciated—it is one of the happiest celebrations that we do.
- Celebrate Math: In our attempt to create a math-rich community at PCIS, with as many Math Across the Curriculum attacks as

possible, we have all 1,400-plus students in the building take part in our monthly "Math Masters" program.

- We also participate in many math competitions for our advanced math students and celebrate Math Month with daily fun math activities and prizes managed by Math Club students. We have a special math awards program in June, with math students receiving recognition for their contributions in the competitions and also in community service. High school math team members come and support these efforts, helping make the transition to high school easier and keeping good math students in our school system.

- Family Math Buddies: I believe in the notion of learning buddies or partners, because it is easy for kids to get lost in a group but not as easy if they have just one partner. We took this a step further in the following way: As part of a grant, we offered families of low-scoring math students the opportunity to come together to work on math homework, math understanding, and positive math attitudes. The catch was that this unique program was for a student and an adult buddy. We were not sure if we would have any takers, but we ended up with about 25 faithful students who came with a parent or guardian in the late afternoons to work on math from January through the end of the year!

- As a school, we celebrate Pi Day (March 14). I realized while running after school one day that I really did not know what pi meant. I decided to hold a student contest to have students explain to me what pi was and what it meant in math. I did wanted posters and got the parent group to offer some small prizes (like school store certificates and a couple of $25 mall certificates). I figured somebody might be willing to explain pi to his or her principal. I had hundreds of participants and had to hold several rounds, each involving a nice conversation. I got to know lots of kids (in a school of 1,450 to 2,100, that is always a challenge). My walks out to bus dismissal became academic conversations, and the finalists did incredible presentations (cartoons, scripts, displays). It was a great connection and one more chance to have kids, families, and teachers share the learning and teaching with students!

It's Not Your Mom's Detention Anymore:
A Study on the Effectiveness of
Walking for Fitness as an Alternative
to Traditional Afterschool Detention*

Marilyn Svaluto
Southgate, Michigan

In the United States, 42% of teenagers are overweight, and 65% of those are categorized as obese. Obesity is considered by the American Heart Association as one of the nation's most pressing health challenges facing Americans. Incidents of heart related disease and debilitating injury in adults less than 55 years of age has increased 50% in the last 25 years. Overweight teenagers are four times more likely to develop diabetes than average weight counterparts. Overweight teens miss school twice as often as average weight students. Overweight adults miss work five times more often than average weight adults. Despite laws that discourage it, overweight adults continue to be discriminated against in the workplace.

The Michigan Governor's Council on Youth Fitness has found a direct correlation between physical fitness instruction and student achievement. Women who exercise vigorously in their teens have an 80% less risk of developing breast cancer. Detroit has the dubious distinction of being named the Nation's Fattest City. In addition to these very alarming statistics, the American Medical Association released in May 2004, a study that states that in the last twenty years, teenagers with high blood pressure and related cardiovascular problems have increased by more than 35%. The AMA cites weight, sedentary lifestyle, and poor eating habits as the contributing factors. Further, Johns Hopkins University is concerned about the rising rates of obesity among teens and has recommended that teens reduce meat intake once a week and walk a minimum of three miles per week. Michael O'Shea, Ph.D of the American College of Sports Medicine, recently wrote that adults must set an example for kids to be more active. Citing a July 2003 study at Brigham Young University, Dr. Susan Vincent stated that on average, kids in the United States took 2000 fewer steps daily than their counterparts in Australia and Sweden.

*This is a reprint of an article previously published in *The Bulletin*, August 2004, Vol. 46, No. 1, pp. 16–18, a publication of the Michigan Association of Secondary School Principals. Permission to reprint was obtained from Dr. Douglas McCall, editor, on 6/6/05.

In March 2004, the Detroit Free Press ran a series on Unhealthy Michigan that noted that obesity in Michigan cost residents $3 billion a year. It threatens personal well-being, business productivity and even the economy. Further, Michigan is third in the nation in the percentage of medical expenses relating to obesity. Only Alaska and surprisingly, The District of Columbia, were higher. Many factors contribute to these statistics in Michigan. These include weather, easy access to unhealthy food, and a lack of recreational opportunities. A May 16, 2004 article in the *Oakland Press* states that Obesity is a Global Problem, and that the rising obesity rates reflect changes in the world's diet and lifestyle. In this article, the writer points out that the reduction of as few as 100 calories a day will translate into a loss of 10 pounds a year. However, a modest increase in walking over riding, will net the same result. In the wake of all of this, it seems that schools have the obligation to teach students about fitness and to provide a format for students to become or remain fit.

At Davidson Middle School in Southgate, Michigan, a Carol White Foundation PEP grant provided just such an opportunity. In addition to course work offered through the Physical Education and Health classes, the building principal decided to incorporate some of the newly purchased technology into the after school detention program. The intent of the new format is to find something measurable yet functional for the kids to do when detained after school. For those infractions that would normally detain a student and require that student to sit quietly and be monitored by a detention supervisor, the students would now become involved in a personal fitness experience. Students would be actively improving their health, instead of sitting glassy eyed and drooling during the duration of detention. On January 26, 2004, a memo was sent to all staff explaining the new format of detention and inviting the staff to make use of it as appropriate. On January 27, the first group of "detainees" was introduced to the Walking for Fitness Detention (WF-2). By Thursday, May 13, over 135 students had served the WF-2 detention and completed the evaluation form.

The results have been an overwhelming success. The "punitive" part of an after school detention is the missing of social time with friends on the way home. When kids must remain after school and make their own arrangements to get home, that is the punishment. The question then becomes: What is the most effective use of the time spent after school? While the kids did not like being detained, they did like the required physical activity. A key component of the success of this project was the use of Polar Heart Rate Monitors purchased through the PEP Grant.

The monitor became the detention supervisor. Students had to elevate their heart rate into the Target Zone (TZ) and keep it there for the assigned time. If a student attempted to slack off, the watch would not credit time in the TZ. A student could be physically present for 40 or more minutes, but only record 15 TZ minutes. The requirement was 35 minutes in the Target Zone for the "first timers," with a five minute incremental increase thereafter. Less than eight students were "repeat offenders." In our "gadget oriented" culture, this kind of detention is not likely to be successful unless heart monitors are used and the principal or detention supervisor walks as well. Perhaps the real value of using heart monitors is that students compete only against themselves. Students in peak physical condition had to exert more effort to reach their TZ and stay there; while students who are out of shape attained the TZ rather easily.

However, it became readily apparent who was out of shape; and this often became the basis for discussions during the walks. When the "watch" not the teacher, indicated that the student needed to improve his or her fitness level; it was not a judgment, it was a fact. As parents were informed of the format of this detention, most had no objection to their child's participation. Parents, when informed of the rationale for this detention style, were supportive of its intent. In the surveys of parents of students who received detention, parents stated that they liked the corre-lation "between the punishment and the crime." If a kid was missing an assignment, an "academic detention" was warranted; but for truancy or tardiness, or hall misbehavior, the fitness detention seemed more appro-priate. Many parents were aware that their child does not get sufficient exercise and liked this opportunity to remediate misbehavior and simul-taneously improve fitness. After the students served a detention, they would complete an evaluation.

The responses, while varied, were overwhelmingly positive. They did not like being required to remain after school, missing the bus and social time; but they either liked or "did not mind" walking for fitness and attain-ing their target zone. Most kids said that a WF-2 detention was a deterrent to the misbehavior because of the punitive nature of detention. While the term deterrent was unfamiliar, the concept was not. Most said that it became a learning experience because they found out things about fitness that they did not know. In casual observation, the students seemed less hostile to WF-2 as a consequence to misbehavior.

The teachers' survey responses were also very positive. Perhaps some recognized that they no longer carried the burden of tardiness or hall mis-behavior detention. Others saw it as a new approach to an age old prob-lem. Still others were glad to see the kids engaged in doing something measurable, and not just sitting idly passing time. They saw it as a healthy response to the obesity epidemic in our State. One teacher saw it as a way to promote lifelong fitness habits. The teaching staff did not want this to be the only format for detention. They still wished to retain the option of a "homework style" detention for academic infractions; and those were served with the assigning teacher. The WF-2 detentions were typically assigned for those nonclassroom issues usually under the aegis of the building administrator. As such, all teachers were aware of the WF-2 detention, but many did not assign students to it.

Perhaps the most pleasantly unanticipated response came from a few teachers who asked to be part of the process next year. The suggestion was that if a teacher assigned a WF-2 detention, then the teacher walks with the kid. The teacher would be setting a proper example, but could also use the time to positively interact with the student to remediate the misbehavior. Every responding teacher wants WF-2 to continue next school year. Even the physical education teacher, who feared a correlation between a WF-2 detention and a dislike for exercise, saw the value of WF-2 and would like it to continue. Lifelong fitness and wellness and positive behavior modification can be achieved in the same educational initiative.

Educators have long recognized the direct correlation between a fit and well student population and high student achievement. They do not have to be mutually exclusive. While it is important to teach kids how to spell myocardial infarction and cardiac episode, and to understand what they are, it is imperative to prevent them in their future. The Walking for Fitness Detention program at Davidson Middle School is a big step in the right direction toward achieving that goal.

SNAPSHOTS

Reward Systems Work

Andy Adams
Ava, Missouri

Reward systems work. When we started offering rewards to the students in our building for good work on our state achievement testing, our scores started to climb. Students who scored proficient or who raised their score from one level on previous testing to the next higher level were given admission to a movie at the local theater, along with complimentary soda and popcorn.

Reading Is Important at Every Level

Marla S. Brady
Boca Raton, Florida

Our entire schedule is built around a 90-minute block for reading in Grades K through 5, with a reading class required for students in Grades 6 and 7. Our teachers have all participated in staff development for the teaching of reading. Regardless of a child's grade level, if students enter the school reading below grade level, we have to take them where they are and push them to their potential. Likewise, if they are efficient readers and are reading above grade level, we must provide enriching opportunities. That includes reading in math, reading in social studies, reading in science, and reading in the elective courses. Reading crosses all boundaries, and therefore, all teachers need to understand the fundamentals of teaching reading.

Balanced Literacy Programs

Stewart Carey
Westfield, New Jersey

The sixth- through eighth-grade language arts and reading program at Roosevelt School encompasses balanced literacy. At each grade, the skills and mechanics of grammar, usage and various forms of literature, poetry, writing, and public speaking are integrated. All students enroll in a separate public speaking course for two years that focuses on articulation, clarity, eye contact, and coherent content.

The Westfield Writing Process is part of our writing program. Students across the curriculum process writing to think, refine, and produce final products. They learn to use peer editing as a way to grow in their ability to become accomplished writers.

Reading is an important part of our program. Students read in all areas of the curriculum. Specifically, in language arts, they read authentic literature in many different genres. This wide array of literature gives them an opportunity to experience authors and styles of writing that stretch them as young readers. In addition, students are required to read a novel of their own selection each month.

A very small number of students test below grade level in reading. These students are supported by the regular classroom teacher and also by special-education teachers who target specific skills in comprehension and vocabulary. Students may also have a special reading class that is offered by a trained reading teacher.

Focus Reading and Focus Math

Susan G. Curtis
Franklin, Tennessee

In our middle school, students have 60 minutes of daily instruction in math, language arts, science, and social studies. They also have two related arts periods each day. During one of these related arts periods, students go back to math or language arts for a nine-week period of what we call Focus Reading or Focus Math. We schedule these groups with students whose reading levels or math levels are approximately the same. Thus, if the group needs remedial work, it is provided, or if it is enrichment the group needs, then a different approach is taken. Students are thereby offered an extra nine weeks of reading and an extra nine weeks of math in small groups of 10 to 12 students. Math and science teachers teach the Focus Math groups, whereas language arts and social studies teachers teach the Focus Reading groups.

An Inspiring Fine Arts Program

Stewart Carey
Westfield, New Jersey

Roosevelt School has a fine arts program that is truly inspiring. We offer comprehensive art and music courses to sixth and seventh graders and the opportunity to take a full year of art, music, or drama in eighth grade. One hundred percent of all sixth- and seventh-grade students are enrolled in the arts, and an overwhelming majority of eighth-grade students are enrolled in the arts. Westfield's rich tradition of supporting the arts can be seen in the murals in the hallways of our school, the artwork that is shared with our local merchants during Youth Art Month, and the artwork on school program covers, assignment books, and school publications—all of which are created by our own student artists. Numerous students have won local, state, and regional contests in art, music, and drama as a result of the high level of instruction, a committed staff, and dedicated and talented students.

Roosevelt has audition ensembles that meet before school two to three days per week. Students in seventh and eighth grade who meet the criteria can be part of a morning orchestra, jazz band, or a premier choral group. These groups are challenged with advanced repertoire, and several concerts are held throughout the year. Also, our student groups routinely perform for outside organizations and institutions.

A highly regarded fall drama and full-scale spring musical further enhance our fine arts program. Students in our extracurricular "Thespian Troupe" successfully participate in forensics competitions in various districts throughout the state.

We have a decade-long tradition of presenting a fine arts day. Throughout the day, student talent in music, art, and drama is showcased on stage. Parents, members of the community, and students alike enjoy this daylong showcasing of talent. We believe that the school support and commitment given to this student-centered program go a long way to including all of our students, providing unique opportunities for them to perform and demonstrate their talents, and, at the same time, helping to improve scores in other academic areas.

Exploration Classes

Stan Beiner
Atlanta, Georgia

Based on Renzulli's (1977) model, the Epstein School made room in its schedule for middle school students to explore interests with their teachers. To do so, the school eliminated one rotation (arts/drama) and an elective or study hall. Academies meet for extended periods weekly. Often, teachers conduct academies in which they are not experts; they are on a journey to learn as well. Parents have also been engaged as facilitators allowing for such diverse offerings as Israeli dance, woodworking, rock and roll band, and mural art. Fourth and fifth graders have a similar program of electives, although the structure is a bit more formal. This program allows for students and teachers to form stronger relationships. It is considered one of the highlights of each year for most middle school students.

Math Newsletter

Lyman Goding
Plymouth, Massachusetts

At PCIS, our motto was "We're all about learning." We emphasized continuous improvement in math in our newsletter. For example, one math issue included "10 ways to show your kids that you care about math," information on how to become "math literate," and an article from the *Boston Globe* that talked about parental math anxiety and its potential impact on math teaching and learning for students. This same newsletter included information from surveying 20 straight-A math students for ideas, tips, or secrets that families could use to help with math. Some of those ideas included: Study with your children, but don't give them the answers; remind students that there is no such thing as a "stupid question"; and teach children to always check their answers just as they would proofread their writing. Another article in the newsletter listed six ways to have fun doing math at home, math Web sites, and homework help resources.

Developing Student Leadership

Stan Beiner
Atlanta, Georgia

Rather than create a typical student council format in the elementary school, the staff created a new vision in which all students should be able to experience leadership and have a role in shaping their community. On the first day of school, fifth graders participate in leadership training activities and learn what to expect for the year. They learn about responsibility from community leaders, participate in a ropes course (teamwork), and then choose a committee to work on for the remainder of the year. Representatives from each committee meet with the principal of the elementary school to discuss issues. Committees include

- facilities improvement,
- peer coaching,
- communications, and
- school spirit.

The message to the students is that everyone has a role to play in the leadership process, whether one is a chair or an active committee member. Although it is not in place yet, we are working toward involving our sixth through eighth graders in a similar leadership experience.

Summary

Curriculum and Instruction Research: Involve teachers in directing instructional improvement, promote student learning, stay informed of effective instructional practices, encourage and support teachers, model good practice, monitor teaching, continually dialogue with others, and recognize academic excellence.

Best Practices for Curriculum and Instruction From Award-Winning Secondary School Principals

- Promote student learning
- Encourage authentic student work
- Emphasize standards
- Build curriculum to fit student needs
- Allow students to explore personal and career interests
- Use a variety of instructional strategies
- Emphasize reading
- Provide remediation when needed
- Celebrate academics
- Reward achievement
- Provide resources
- Share responsibility and accountability
- Consider looping
- Look for evidence of achievement
- Monitor results

CURRICULUM AND INSTRUCTIONAL PROGRAMS REFLECTION

1. What are the effective instructional programs at our school?

2. What are the strengths and weaknesses of the instructional programs at our school?

3. What am I doing to support the instructional programs at our school?

4. How can I support the instructional program better?

5. In what ways does our curriculum prepare students for lifelong learning?

6. Which ideas in this chapter would be a good fit for our school?

7. How can we implement these ideas in our school?

8. How might we need to revise these ideas for them to be successful on our campus?

ADDITIONAL RESOURCES

Achievement Gap
http://www.education.ky.gov/KDE/Instructional+Resources/Closing+the+Gap

Advancement Via Individual Determination
http://www.avidonline.org

American Heart Association
http://www.americanheart.org

American Medical Association
http://www.ama-assn.org

Center for Effective Collaboration and Practice–University of Oregon
http://cecp.air.org

Commonwealth Accountability Testing System—Kentucky Accountability Test
http://www.education.ky.gov/KDE

Creating Independence through Student-owned Strategies
http://www.crec.org/tabs/special/criss.html

Delaware Student Testing Program
http://www.doe.state.de.us/aab

Effective Behavior Support
http://cecp.air.org

Extended Learning Time
http://www.ed.gov/legislation/ESEA/sec10993.html

Gaining Early Awareness and Readiness for Undergraduate
Programs (GEAR UP)
http://www.ed.gov/programs/gearup/index.html

Global Learning and Observations to Benefit the Environment
http://www.globe.gov

Knowledge Masters competitions
http://www.greatauk.com

Looping
http://www.ncrel.org

Math Across the Curriculum
http://www.unr.edu/mathcenter/mac

MathCounts
http://mathcounts.org

Michigan's Governor's Council on Youth Fitness
http://www.michiganfitness.org

National Middle School Association
http://www.nmsa.org

Positive Attitudes Create Success
http://www.positivethinkingaffirmations.com

Pre–Standardized Aptitude Test
http://www.princetonreview.com/college/testprep

Professional Learning Community
http://www.sedl.org/pubs/change34

REFERENCES

DuFour, R. & Eaker, R. (1998). *Professional learning communities at work: Best practices for enhancing student achievement.* Bloomington, IN: National Educational Service.

Feds say 45 area schools fail to make the grade. (2005, August 12). *San Antonio Express News*, 6A.

Hoy, A., & Hoy, W. (2003). *Instructional leadership: A learning-centered guide.* Boston: Allyn & Bacon.

Marzano, R. J., Pickering, D. J., & Pollock, J. E. (2001). *Classroom instruction that works.* Alexandria, VA: Association of Supervision and Curriculum Development.

Renzulli, J. S. (1977). *The enrichment triad model.* Mansfield Center, CT: Creative Learning Press.

Southworth, G. (2005). Learning-centered leadership. In B. Davies (Ed.), *The essentials of school leadership* (pp. 75–92). Thousand Oaks, CA: Corwin Press.

Starratt, R. (2005). Ethical leadership. In B. Davies (Ed.), *The essentials of school leadership* (pp. 61–74). Thousand Oaks, CA: Corwin Press.

CHAPTER FIVE

School Improvement Plans

> Learning lies at the heart of school leadership and improvement.
> —*Southworth (2005, p. 86)*

Just when we think we have learned everything there is to know, we hear of a good idea and often say, "Why didn't I think of that?" Will Durant, author and historian, wrote, "60 years ago I knew everything; now I know nothing. Education is a progressive discovery of our own ignorance" (as cited in Blaydes, 2003, p. 143). One of the strengths that effective principals bring to leadership is this acknowledgment that we will never learn everything that there is to learn. In fact, the more we know, generally, the more we realize there is for us to know. Thus, we become lifelong learners as we continue to seek another good idea, another best practice. But the very practice of continuing to seek knowing more about our craft causes us to grow. As Oliver Wendell Holmes said, "Man's mind stretched to a new idea never goes back to its original dimensions" (see http://www.brainyquote.com).

School improvement does not happen without change. Yet, although it is important for principals to initiate change on a campus, being able to nurture and sustain that change is critical for lasting school improvement (Harris, 2004). Fullan (2001) even suggested that it does not matter how personally committed to school improvement principals are; without the support and commitment of the faculty and the larger school community, improvement is doomed to fail. Although school improvement is accomplished to some degree by changing policies, procedures, and curricula, when it is personal and transformative, it has the power to change lives.

Lambert (2003) called this *capacity building*, and it involves teaching, learning, and leading.

Capacity-building principals believe that school improvement is accomplished when all faculty participate in accomplishing a shared vision of schools in which everyone is a learner. This is characterized by a collaborative environment in which everyone shares in the leadership as well as accepts the responsibility for seeing that all students achieve. Building leadership capacity fosters school improvement through establishing a culture of inquiry that is based on systematically and continually asking the right questions, collecting and considering evidence (data), and creating student learning goals that emphasize creating new understandings as a result of this process (Lambert, 2003; Southworth, 2005). Consequently, the principal becomes the learning leader on the campus. In this capacity, principals implementing school reform and improvement strategies emphasize the following practices:

- encourage individualized instruction,
- look at the data,
- expand the school schedule to involve new configurations,
- focus on curriculum articulation and alignment,
- improve student-centered strategies, and
- involve parents in more ways. (Bushman, Goodman, Brown-Welty, & Dorn, 2001)

Because school improvement is such a far-reaching topic, the best practices in this chapter run the gamut from understanding data analysis to providing training for bus drivers, all of which contribute to school improvement. First, Dorothy Garrison-Wade points out that the very process of school improvement improves us all through its transformative power. Evelyn Ennsmann describes the collaborative Target, Explore, Apply, Modify, and Share cycle, whereas Tom Hamilton shares the impact of *Breaking Ranks II* (2004) on school improvement. Other best practice ideas in this chapter emphasize school improvement as a result of capacity building through collaboration and professional development.

The last entry in this chapter is from award-winning principal Shirley Johnson. Johnson was principal of 1 of the original 10 high schools in Ted Sizer's (1992) Coalition of Essential Schools nearly 25 years ago. She is a recognized leader in education. Although it is our hope that readers will incorporate many of the best practices in this book to improve schools for student learning, even more than that, we are concerned that schools become effective and *stay* effective. For that reason, I asked Johnson to reflect on her experiences in education and share her best practices for nurturing and sustaining school improvement ideas to promote student learning.

School Improvement Improves Us All

Dorothy Garrison-Wade
Wilmington, North Carolina

I believe in children. My love for children, coupled with a strong desire to spark young minds, led me into the field of education. I believe every child is entitled to learn something new each day in school. This may sound like an arduous task for some, but I feel that learning something new each day is the minimum level of educational commitment to which our children are entitled.

As a former school administrator with 13 years of leadership experience (3 years as a principal, 4 years as an assistant principal, and 6 years as a school administrator in the private sector), I fulfilled this commitment by providing instructional leadership to inspire and motivate teachers to offer learning opportunities that address the individual needs of each student. Whenever I observed a teacher using one approach to address the needs of all children in his or her classroom, it became my job as building principal to provide professional development to help the teacher discover differentiated teaching strategies. Once children are viewed as individuals and not as a large group, learning occurs. You can easily observe the enthusiasm and excitement on a child's face when he or she knows the teacher views him or her as an individual. After 22 years as an educator, I still get excited every time I see the "ah, I get it" expression on a child's face.

The only way for an administrator to be a part of the excitement of the learning process is to have firsthand knowledge of what is going on in his or her school by being a visible presence in the school. As a former principal, I perceived it was my responsibility to know what was going on in my school and lead by modeling. Throughout the day, I interacted by being positive and cheerful with staff and students in the classroom and hallways. I observed or participated in classroom instruction; attended grade level meetings, student support meetings, and departmental meetings;

conducted staff development training; and met with parents to problem solve and develop strategies that aided in enhancing students' achievement. I acknowledged the achievements of others by writing notes, giving gifts, and making public recognition.

My First Principalship

My first building-level principalship assignment was at Trask Middle School (TMS), an urban school with a student enrollment of approximately 1,000 students. As principal, my leadership style was very participatory. I led by example and by establishing high priorities for spending time in the instructional setting. I viewed my role as principal as a guide, a coach, and a facilitator of learning. I did this by collaborating with my staff to develop a school improvement plan aligned with our school's goals, district's goals, and state standards. The main intent was to improve student achievement by encouraging every child to strive for academic excellence. I found it important to get firsthand knowledge and stay attuned to what my teachers were experiencing each day by teaching and modeling the desired behavior. As a result, I constantly assessed instructional programs to determine the best strategies and approaches to enhance students' achievement.

One of the most rewarding experiences I had at TMS was teaching a group of 13 students in a program called Positive Attitudes Create Success (P.A.C.S.). Some of the topics presented in P.A.C.S. sessions included conflict resolution, social skills, relationships, interpersonal skills, and test-taking strategies. These students were recommended by their teachers as at risk in the educational environment. I saw my P.A.C.S. students daily in various educational settings. They knew I observed their behavior, monitored their grades and attendance, and established high expectations for their success. Twice a month, I met formally with them and conducted lessons to help them be successful in the school setting. In addition, I took my students on field trips so they could get firsthand experience. I know I have made a positive difference to my group, as it is evident when they come to me to avoid getting in trouble and by their improved academic progress (75% academically involved performance of P.A.C.S. students). By working with P.A.C.S. members, not only did I get a rewarding opportunity to work closely with students, but teachers got an opportunity to observe me working directly with students with various academic, social, and behavioral problems. Some other steps I took at TMS to achieve the school's goals included

- establishing an afterschool tutoring program for students needing help;
- creating encore and remediation classes for students not meeting state standards in reading, writing, and mathematics on end-of-grade assessments;
- creating a SUCCESS program for students unsuccessful in regular classroom settings, including individualized instruction to improve deficit areas and counseling sessions with students to develop social skills, study and test-taking skills, and conflict resolution strategies;
- encouraging high expectations and reviewing teachers' nine-week lesson plans for alignment with the standard course of study;
- encouraging teachers to pursue National Board certification, resulting in four teachers receiving National Board certification during my tenure;
- conducting "Best Teaching Practices" and quality teacher training to enhance instruction;
- using technology to promote student achievement, serving on the school's technology team, and offering afterschool tutoring to eighth graders to prepare them for the state computer competency test;
- receiving training from the Principals' Executive Program at the University of North Carolina, Chapel Hill, in technology leadership, and also receiving training at North Carolina Teaching Academy focusing on integrating technology into education; and
- developing a character education committee in conjunction with the guidance department to promote positive character traits.

My efforts to improve our school were acknowledged by the district when I was selected as the 2001–2002 New Hanover County Schools' Principal of the Year. To receive this award, one must be nominated by fellow principals, endure an extensive interview, and develop a professional portfolio.

My Second Principalship

My second building-level leadership role was a combined job as principal of Lakeside High School and director of the Alternative Pathways for Success programs. This position gave me experience in working with a diverse school community. Specifically, I managed an inner-city alternative high school and three additional special academic programs (Alternative Pathways for Success, Middle School Pathways, and a transition program for young adults). At Lakeside, it was vital that I collaborate with staff members to create and maintain a school climate conducive to learning. I took similar steps as those taken at TMS to improve students' achievement. I also encouraged professional growth for staff aligned with state standards and our school's goals. At Lakeside, I provided my staff with numerous professional opportunities to accomplish goals. We had monthly staff development activities to improve technology skills and teaching strategies. In addition, I encouraged teachers to receive National Board certification. When I left Lakeside, three teachers were pursuing board certification.

As a firm believer of the importance of direct contact with students, I formed a multicultural reading club. The club was called "multicultural reading" because the students were primarily students of color and the book selections mainly focused on multicultural topics. The students chose many selections, including

- *The Color of Water* by James McBride,
- *The Bluest Eye* by Toni Morrison,
- *Faces at the Bottom of the Well* by Derrick Bell,
- *Makes Me Wanna Holler* by Nathan McCall,
- *In Search of Satisfaction* by J. California Cooper, and
- *I Know Why the Caged Bird Sings* by Maya Angelou.

As the club's leader, I met bimonthly with students to discuss book selections and took students on field trips to the library and museum. As a schoolwide incentive, we offered students in the school a no-cost field trip to spend three nights in Charleston, South Carolina. One major requirement of the trip was that students had to maintain a C or better average to qualify. For many students, this was a major incentive because many of them had never been out of the state. This project required me to solicit money from district and community organizations. The Rotary Club ultimately gave us $10,000 to sponsor the trip.

Having the opportunity to work with P.A.C.S. members, multicultural reading groups, and other students was the most rewarding part of my job as principal. Enthusiasm, motivation, and passion for knowledge were the gifts I offered my students. As a facilitator of learning, I challenged my students to explore, to achieve the impossible, and to seek the "why" and "how." In turn, I continued to learn and explore with them. Together, we opened new doors and explored uncharted ideas, thus facilitating their intellectual growth and progression toward self-actualization.

What I Wish I Had Done Differently

Dorothy Garrison-Wade
Wilmington, North Carolina

In July 1999, I drove up to TMS. I could not believe that my dream of becoming a building-level principal was finally a reality. I was so excited and very enthusiastic when I entered the office. I will never forget the cheerful expression of my head secretary as I introduced myself to her. As she escorted me to my office, I was surprised to see papers and various documents all over the floor and table in the office. But even the disarray of my new office was not going to snuff out my excitement. That day, I dived into determining what steps to take in organizing my office and completing the various reports that were left behind from the previous administrator.

My first objective was to assess the environment to find out all I could about TMS's teachers and students. Initially, I called the previous administrator for background information, but he was not available, as he had already left town. My challenge would be more difficult than I had originally imagined. Next, I talked with one of the assistant principals to attain relevant information. She was very candid in her perception of the school's strengths and weaknesses. She informed me I might encounter resistance due to the inflexibility of many of the staff to change. In the same meeting, she informed me the master schedule had not been completed, several major reports were due, there were three teacher vacancies, and she was seeking other employment. My challenge was just beginning, and I did not have a clue what other obstacles I would encounter, but I knew I was on a mission to make a difference for my children.

Next, I met with all the department chairs to discuss what they perceived as the school's strengths and weaknesses. They were very informative and appeared to freely share information about TMS. That was when I made my first major mistake. You see, I was so eager to fix the problems, I did not take enough time to observe the school culture and environment.

As the school year ensued, I quickly realized my mistake—I had moved too quickly. Although I was cautioned to take it slowly in making changes, I proceeded with what I thought was a slow pace, but in hindsight, the pace was not slow enough for a school that had already experienced a great deal of change by having four different principals in a six-year time span. When I told the staff of my idea to have an afterschool tutoring program to help students, I did not think it would cause such discontentment. All teachers were asked to develop a schedule in their department or grade level to have a teacher on duty for one hour after school, three times a week, to provide academic assistance to the students. In most cases, an individual teacher would only be committed to tutor after school two times a month. Although, for me, this request was a reasonable expectation for teachers performing additional duties, many teachers did not agree.

I could have avoided this and other problems encountered during my first year by taking time to learn about the educational community. I was still very enthusiastic about the opportunity I had each day to provide instructional leadership. I learned many valuable lessons during my first year. I realized I must be patient and not expect change to occur overnight. I tried to involve all stakeholders in the decision-making process. Students, parents, and teachers served on our site-based team. I consulted with the site-based team in making major program changes. Shared decision making is essential for continuous improvement and for the members to accept ownership of and have pride in their school.

Although my expectations were still very high, I realized that my vision for the school must be a shared vision of all the stakeholders. Hopefully, by modeling strong work ethics, good character, a passion for education, a willingness to assist wherever needed, and a desire for all children to learn, I provided the instructional leadership needed for my school to accomplish our mission. Patience is a virtue.

Everyone Is Accountable for All

Andy Adams
Ava, Missouri

It is important to establish a system that holds all teachers in your building accountable for the welfare of all the students. I believe this happens as a result of strong leadership in each building. I started day one of my principalship by telling all the staff that we were all responsible for the successes and failures of our students all the way through their educational careers and that the foundation we established in middle school would determine, ultimately, the success of our students in later years. When we met in professional development meetings, we would divide all teachers of math, language arts, science, and so forth into groups, all the way from fifth through eighth grade. By doing this, the teachers became familiar with each other, the curricula in other grade levels, and established areas that they were responsible for in teaching their class. Not all items tested in eighth grade are learned in eighth grade. Students have to have a basis and foundation for the years prior to that level.

I remember when our eighth-grade scores went down a bit a few years ago. We were discussing this in a faculty meeting, and one of our fifth-grade teachers spoke up and said, "What are we doing wrong in fifth grade that the scores went down in eighth? Tell us what we need to do and we will do it, because we are as responsible for these kids in eighth grade as we are in the fifth grade." I was fortunate that I had a staff who believed in this message and in the welfare of all of our students. You can see why I loved this staff so much!

TEAMS Target Improved Student Learning

Evelyn Ennsmann
Villa Park, Illinois

School improvement at Willowbrook High School is a collaborative effort in which staff development is especially important. Our staff development committee is composed of district leadership; Audrey Haugan, former assistant superintendent of curriculum and instruction (committee chair); our building leadership team; and our teacher-leaders. Our purpose is to serve as a resource for high school departments in following the Target, Explore, Apply, Modify, and Share (TEAMS) cycle in our district. The TEAMS cycle is the process that we use in District 88, presented as a process and then implemented due to this collaborative effort of leadership by Haugan, our teacher union, teacher-leaders, and the building leadership team. Haugan, myself, and Scott Helton (principal of our sister school) presented at the No Child Left Behind conference in 2004 in Chicago on how we use the TEAMS cycle as a process to continue to revise and change our department goals to meet the needs of our students.

As principal, I work with the committee to provide focus, leadership, and direction in implementing two goals by the year 2007. Goal One is to have students engaged in curricula that incorporate increased integrated thinking and application experiences. Goal Two is to provide time and resources for professional growth and development programs that ensure that the entire staff has the skills and knowledge to enhance learning goals and meet student needs. The TEAMS cycle covers five components to improve student learning (see Figure 5.1).

Led by the work of Audrey Haugan, we have implemented four worksheets to track our progress: Target Goal (Figure 5.2), Evidence of Best Practice and Research (Figure 5.3), Action Plan (Figure 5.4), and Feedback Sheet (Figure 5.5).

Using *Breaking Ranks II* for School Improvement

Tom Hamilton
Bardstown, Kentucky

I was a *Breaking Ranks II* (2004) fan the first time I saw the book. As a high school principal for the past 13 years, I was pretty familiar with the concepts and ideas presented in *Breaking Ranks II,* and with many high school restructuring programs, for that matter. What *Breaking Ranks II* brought was the implementation process. Finally, a how-to book with models and real-world examples for high school restructuring was available. When I found out about the National Association of Secondary School Principals/Gates Grant to train national leaders in *Breaking Ranks II,* I volunteered to be one of a three-member team to write an application for Kentucky. Kentucky, in turn, was 1 of the 13 states to win a grant, and I was a member of a five-person team to train in Providence, Rhode Island.

I was particularly interested in the professional development aspect of *Breaking Ranks II* (2004). I knew that the most important school improvement plans were not in structures, programs, or schedules (important as they are), but in the classrooms! We had to have embedded and ongoing training for teachers to be successful with diverse cultures and learning styles. Our staff was ready to try something different, and using examples from *Breaking Ranks II,* we completely revamped our professional development. One key

Figure 5.1   TEAMS Cycle

DuPage High School District 88

TEAMS Cycle

Target opportunities to improve student learning.
    Review building goals/objectives
    Data assessment
    Identification of student needs/weaknesses

Examine past practice and current research.
    Modify target areas if necessary.
    Define best practices to meet student needs.
    Consult with others with expertise.
    Divide department into teams as necessary to work on plans.

Apply new knowledge to develop & implement a plan for change.
    Indicate strategies, timeline, and persons involved.
    Identify what "products" might result from the action plan.
    Implement the best practice teaching strategies.
    Implement the plan into classrooms.
    Gather student feedback/input.

Modify plans as necessary.
    Complete work from previous month as necessary.
    Discuss/share lessons and strategies that have worked.
    Discuss/share lessons and strategies that have not been
    successful if applicable.
    Assess results against intended results.
    Develop next steps for implementation of the plan.
    Revise timelines as necessary.
    Share successes on a building level with other departments.

Share evidence of improved student learning.
    Share exemplary models/action plans.
    Discuss implications for school improvement plans and future
    department goals.

ingredient was teaming with our middle school, whose principal was also a big fan of the book. We built instructional leadership teams based on interest across grade levels and sent 18 middle and high school teachers to a national program on best practice teaching techniques based on learning

(Text continues on page 147)

Figure 5.2   TEAMS Target Goal

DuPage High School District 88

GOALS

School: _____   Date: _____

Department: _____

Department Need: (Must address a student weakness)

_____

Evidence of Weakness (3 examples: Student work; local assessments, teacher input, state assessments if applicable):

1. _____

2. _____

3. _____

Evidence of Successes

To what extent will students improve in each of the areas addressed?

1. The percentage of students having success will increase in this area from _____%
   to _____ %.

Explanation:

_____

Other Success Indicators:

_____

2. The percentage of students having success will increase in this area from _____%
   to _____ %.

Explanation:

_____

Other Success Indicators:

_____

(Continued)

Figure 5.2 (Continued)

3. The percentage of students having success will increase in this area from _____%
   to _____ %.

Explanation:

_____

Other Success Indicators:

_____

Figure 5.3   TEAMS Evidence

DuPage High School District 88

Evidence of Best Practice and Research

Department: _____   School: _____

Goal Statement:

_____

1. What evidence of best practices/research have you found as related to the
   improvement of this student weakness? (List several resources including past
   practices, journals, books, authors, teacher accounts, etc.)

_____

_____

2. How does this research match or differ from what you previously thought about
   teaching this goal area?

_____

_____

Figure 5.4   TEAMS Action

DuPage High School District 88

ACTION PLAN

Department: _____   Date: _____

Goal Statement:

_____

Evidence of Best Practice/Research:

_____

_____

Strategies, Timelines, People Involved:
(What will teachers do? What will students do?)

_____

_____

Products:

    How will we know students have improved?
    What assessments will be used?
    What role will students play in charting assessment and monitoring their own
    learning?

_____

_____

Learning

1. What did we as teachers learn about our own teaching as a result of this process?

_____

2. What did we learn about our students?

_____

3. What did we learn about our community of learners?

_____

Figure 5.5   TEAMS Feedback

School: _____   Date: _____

Department: _____

What were the successes and obstacles you encountered in your department in relation to each area? Please be specific in your examples.

Target goal:
Examine past practice/research:
Action plan:
Modify the plan:
Share and celebrate:

Learning

1. What did we as teachers learn about our own teaching as a result of this process?

_____

2. What did we learn about our students?

_____

3. What evidence do we have that supports/refutes our goals? Please attach any supporting information. What were your findings as a result of this year's work?

_____

4. What direction do you see your department going next fall? What goals do you think you will focus on and why?

_____

5. Was the process effective for your department? Please explain why or why not.

_____

styles. The plan was to use these instructional leaders to model and explain these practices in a school setting.

Gone was the professional development plan anchored in expensive outside speakers who spend a day or two with the faculty members getting everyone fired up, only to lose that fire after a week or two of isolation in their closed classrooms. In contrast, we have a professional development plan that is anchored in multiage and content teacher teams that spend planning periods together sharing the success and failures of trying new teaching practices in real classroom settings. It provides support and encouragement from peers in a nonthreatening evaluation process. As the authors of *Breaking Ranks II* (2004) stated, the effectiveness of any professional development plan is first measured by how well your staff likes it. This staff is so enthusiastic about our new plan that they turned down an offer for the instructional leadership team to attend an expensive national conference. Their reason? They did not want to lose momentum on the teaching practices they had already implemented.

The data support their decision. In terms of state accountability scores, Bardstown High School (BHS) meets or exceeds state averages in six out of seven content areas. In 2004, BHS students scored the following: In mathematics, BHS students scored an index of 82.9, the state average was 68.8; in science, BHS students scored 83.9, the state average was 68.3; in social studies, BHS students scored 84.2, the state average was 73.4; in arts and humanities, BHS students scored 79.2, the state average was 72.3; in writing, BHS students scored 68.8, the state average was 65.1; and in reading, BHS students scored 73.3, the state average was 73.8. Only in practical living did BHS students not meet the state average. BHS students scored 77.3; the state average was 79.2. We are working on that! One note: BHS has been above most state averages for the past five years.

New Teacher Mentoring Program

Evelyn Ennsmann
Villa Park, Illinois

At Willowbrook High School, Pete Montgomery, one of our teacher-leaders, works with new teachers, the administration, as well as mentors. The basic design of the mentorship program is for experienced District 88 teachers to work with newly hired staff members as part of a continuous staff development process, including participation in the district's various staff development offerings. Experienced staff who have mastered their craft and are dedicated to promoting excellence and quality in the teaching profession will be sought as mentors for staff new to District 88.

Responsibilities

Mentors play several roles, including guide, role model, sponsor, counselor, coach, resource, and colleague. The protégé is required to attend two half-day new teacher workshops and the full-day District 88 new teacher inservice day in the fall. The mentor is responsible for both assisting the protégé with questions and issues and providing leadership to make the protégé aware of current concepts, materials, practices, and methods in his or her area. At no point is the mentor's role evaluative, but rather collegial.

The mentorship program also provides an opportunity for experienced staff members to grow professionally and advance their careers by sharing their talents and expertise with new staff members. This occurs during the second semester, in part, during preobservation meetings, classroom observations, and postobservation discussions that mentors and protégés participate in. This cycle of observations continues in a second year for the new teacher. In addition, informal meetings between mentor and protégé should take place on at least a weekly basis for questions, feedback, and further suggestions.

Mentors have an opportunity to instill confidence, focus, perspective, and a working knowledge that helps protégés develop self-direction and a sound instructional decision-making process. The opportunity for mentors to be creative and resourceful also exists and is encouraged. The ultimate purpose of the mentorship program is to enhance the instructional climate in District 88 through the help and advice provided by the mentor.

Selection

A selection committee composed of the department chair, building administrators, and mentor coordinators determines the best candidates for mentors. Department chairs cannot be mentor teachers. Interns are not included in the mentoring or induction program and are therefore not assigned a formal mentor. There are no seniority rights to mentoring positions, and selections are based on need each year.

Financial Compensation

Mentors receive a $500 stipend or an hour of credit on the salary schedule for each year they serve as a mentor. In addition, mentors will be paid $100 for one day of mandatory training in the fall. The stipends are not tied to anything else in the contract and will be awarded on an annual basis. A minimum of 16 hours of logged clock hours outside of the contractual school day is required for the credit or stipend. The $500 stipend or credit hour will be awarded on successful completion of mentoring and will be paid at the end of the school year.

How We Use Data Assessment

Dan Stepenosky
Beverly Hills, California

The high school consciously engages in data-driven decision making to improve student and school performance. Assessment data are regularly collected, disseminated, analyzed, and integrated into discussions and planning surrounding improvement of the educational process. These data include grades and results from the California Standardized Testing and Reporting (STAR) tests, PSATs, SAT Reasoning Tests, SAT Subject Tests, Golden State exams, advanced placement (AP) exams, and departmental placement and final exams. We distribute a schoolwide report of student grades by department and generate an underachievers' report each semester for counselors, who contact students and parents to determine appropriate remedies. These reports were the impetus for the creation of a guidance class to assist at-risk students. In addition, teachers have access to individual STAR test results to evaluate the effectiveness of teaching methods and to determine individual student needs. There is a general expectation that the standards-based education provided by every department will produce consistent results on state, school, and classroom assessments. Noted disparities in those assessments trigger an analysis to determine the source of and remedy for the differences.

Teachers also regularly use a wide range of assessment information to improve student achievement of standards. The administration annually advises teachers of student gifted and talented education, 504, special-education, Reading Plus, and English-learners (EL) designations that may affect the student's achievement level. All teachers meet with special-education service providers in October to read their students' individualized education plans and to discuss modifications to instruction and assessment. An EL World History and an EL U.S. History class were created for students in the EL program.

Low STAR reading test results led to the creation of a Reading Plus class to help students improve their reading comprehension. A two-year algebra program was designed for students with undeveloped math skills, and a functions, statistics, and trigonometry course was designed to give another opportunity for entrance into precalculus to students who are strong in mathematics but did not qualify for the advanced math level. In math, the course grade, final exam grade, and teacher recommendations are used to determine student placements. Algebra and Algebra A teachers use the University of California, Los Angeles, Math Diagnostic Test to verify appropriate course placement. English teachers use the STAR test as a component of the honors placement process and the STAR test and the district sophomore writing proficiency exam to identify students requiring remediation in reading and writing.

Using Assessment Data

Stewart Carey
Westfield, New Jersey

All eighth-grade students in New Jersey are tested using the Grade Eight Proficiency Assessment (GEPA). The GEPA consists of tests in language arts literacy, mathematics, and science. The GEPA is designed to test student ability and proficiency in each of these areas. In reporting these standardized testing scores, the New Jersey Department of Education categorizes students as partially proficient, proficient, or advanced proficient in each of these areas. Since the beginning of these tests, our eighth-grade students have had outstanding performance. In each area—science, language arts literacy, and mathematics—a high percentage of our students have scored proficient and advanced proficient.

Assessment data play a critical role in the improvement of classroom instruction. We thoroughly analyze test results provided by New Jersey. Student essays, graded on a scale of one to six, are reviewed by the language arts department. Individual tests are read and the scores analyzed. Data are used to refine classroom instruction. This gives valuable information concerning the adequate preparation of students for testing. State-generated assessment reports and individual test scores are shared with the faculty and community. Teachers in each team and the guidance counselors discuss individual student academic progress to provide support for students in need.

Specific attention is paid by the special-education staff to the results of our special-education students. They make adequate yearly progress, and our special-education and regular-education staff work cooperatively to make sure the key skills these students need to have to perform on these assessments are acquired. Assessment data on districtwide assessment are used to provide a basic skills program for students before school to enhance their skills in language arts, literacy, and math. Although this is a small number of students at Roosevelt School, we are committed to leaving no child behind.

The School Improvement Plan as a Living Document

Heath Morrison
Waldorf, Maryland

Several years ago, the staff of Thomas Stone High School identified top priorities and goals that were based on surveys of staff, students, and the community. As the school improvement plan was being revised, several permanent committees were established around those goals with the expressed purpose of monitoring the implementation of the school improvement plan and laying the groundwork for future school improvement. These committees were established in areas such as ninth grade, testing, minority achievement, technology, professional development, special education, school spirit, and future vision. All teachers serve on the committees of their choice on a monthly basis. These school improvement committees have truly been instrumental in ensuring that the school improvement plan does not simply collect dust but is a living document that lays the foundation for continued improvement.

The fact that all teachers serve on a committee ensures that the entire faculty, and not just a select few, make important decisions. In addition, faculty meetings have been reconfigured to allow time for professional development opportunities and activities devised by these teams. More topics and training have been at the suggestion and leadership of the school improvement teams.

Improving Academic Rigor

Tom Hamilton
Bardstown, Kentucky

Another area that we have concentrated on at BHS is to improve academic rigor. Seven years ago, our AP program produced only a few students who took the test and even fewer who actually scored a three or better. In fact, the only purpose it served was as a pseudo-technique to ensure homogeneous grouping. I led a group of staff members to revamp our AP program. We sent all of our teachers to training, emphasized the importance of taking the tests, replaced a few reluctant teachers, and actively recruited minority and underrepresented groups.

In 1999, we had 124 students in eight AP classes, and fewer than 5% of those were minority students. Of those 124 students, only 23 took the AP test, with four scoring three or better. In 2004, we had 153 students in 10 AP classes, with 14% minority and 55% female. Those students took 101 tests, with 35 of them scoring three or better. We are particularly proud of our chemistry and calculus programs, in which 50% of our AP students scored three or better and more than half of them are female!

Time and space do not permit me to tell you all of the great things happening at BHS. I am somewhat uncomfortable bringing all this attention on myself; however, if it highlights the accomplishments of this staff and school, I am all for it!

FIVE-MINUTE CLASSROOM WALK-THROUGH

Dana Trevethan
Turlock, California

This practice allows me (the principal) and my administrative team to get in and out of 5 to 6 classes per period so that we can potentially observe anywhere from 25 to 40 classes in a given day. The design of our five-minute walk-through combines those components of effective teaching found in *Madeline Hunter's Mastery Teaching* (Hunter, 2004) and in the program "Optimizing School Productivity, Accelerate Learning to Raise Student Achievement" by Data Works Educational Research (see http://www.dataworks-ed.com). Although many teachers were initially hesitant and concerned about this feedback instrument, they have come to appreciate the immediate comments, notes, and consistent observations that are supported. Ironically, teachers now request that the information collected be included in their performance evaluations.

Each five-minute walk-through card (see Figure 5.6) is left on the teacher's desk following the observation, which focuses on the sharing of standards and objectives with students, explicit direct instruction, and consistent checks for understanding, particularly with those students who do not volunteer to share their responses or understanding. As we work to increase students' understanding of state standards, time on task, and student mastery of the subject matter, we have witnessed heightened awareness among our administration, teachers, and students in regard to these effective teaching elements as a result of implementation of the five-minute walk-through.

TEACHER OBSERVATIONS

Kevin Fillgrove
Ephrata, Pennsylvania

In her book *Enhancing Professional Practice: A Framework for Teaching,* Charlotte Danielson (1996) identified 22 components of good, quality teaching. The 22 components are divided into four domains: planning,

Figure 5.6   Five-Minute Walk-Through Card

Five-Minute Walk-Through Class Visitation

Teacher _____

Date _____

Period _____

Course _____

☐   Posted/Stated Objective

☐   Standards-Aligned

☐   Grade-Level Curriculum

☐   Checking for Understanding (volunteer/non)

☐   (volunteer/non)

☐   (volunteer/non)

☐   Explaining/Modeling/Demonstrating

☐   Guided Practice

☐   Closure

Comments:

_____

_____

_____

_____

Administrator:

_____

preparation, responsibility, and individual work on the part of teachers and administrators.

For observation purposes, I follow strategic steps to enhance the effectiveness of each observation. First, for every observation, teachers submit written responses for planning questions to submit to me before having a preobservation conference. The conference lasts 5 to 30 minutes, during which we discuss various topics. Then, teachers complete a 20- to 40-minute reflection questionnaire. For example, a portion of the questionnaire allows the teacher to reflect on what he or she felt was the most successful part of the lesson taught. This questionnaire is completed before the postobservation. Within 24 hours of observation, teachers complete Danielson's (1996) rubric, which includes 22 criteria. Finally, the teachers and I follow the criteria and discuss ways that will enable them to move from a proficient to a distinguished teacher.

KNOW YOUR FACILITY BETTER THAN ANYONE

Tommy Floyd
Somerset, Kentucky

It is the principal's responsibility to know the facility better than anyone on campus. Therefore, use your time in the beginning to learn where everything is located. This means you find every breaker box, alarm panel, fire alarm pull station, lockable door, and storage closet. Determine where every area of lockers is located, and map their numbers on a computer for easy access. Prepare a detailed building map for emergency purposes. Determine where your traffic congestion locations are and work to solve them. Always arrange for all of your students to arrive in areas where there is adequate supervision at all times. Here are some other best practices to follow:

- Tell teachers that with the exception of dedicated labs and so forth, no rooms are sacred, and for the sake of traffic, student use, and so forth, anyone may be moved from year to year.
- Travel with your students in between classes, be seen, never be at the same location twice, make sure all locked areas are locked, and work to prevent teachers from letting students have access to keys without supervision.

- No matter how good your instructional program, sports teams, Commonwealth Accountability Testing System scores, and so forth are, no one will care if your bathrooms smell like urine or smoke and your building is dirty.
- Make custodial supervision a daily issue, or you might be ignoring a building that could be cleaner—look (at edges, filters, windows, corners, etc.)! Remember, you determine how clean the facility will be, just like you determine everything else.
- Take care of your custodians; include them in everything possible through school promotions. They deserve and respond better to positives than negatives.
- Get a second opinion on the cleaning load (expectations) for all of your custodians. Try to get the most out of them without expecting them to clean too much. Once established, make them stick to it.
- Your grounds, flowerbeds, bushes, trees, signs, and so forth tell every passerby that you do or do not care about what goes on inside the building.
- Your building needs to be the showplace for your district regardless of how long it has been there. Transfer an enormous amount of personal pride to students, staff, and the public.

NURTURING AND SUSTAINING
BEST PRACTICES FOR SCHOOL IMPROVEMENT

Shirley Johnson
Huntsville, Texas

Change in public schools comes slowly and cautiously. As a young principal in the late 1970s and 1980s feeling that we were not appropriately serving students, I aspired to change how high schools organized to deliver student-centered instruction. Today, it is humbling to admit that I was naïve about what it would really take to make significant changes in the way we enabled students to learn at the high school level. Coaching the redesign of high schools today, as a university professor, I have a different perspective as to what should be done to accomplish a mission of such magnitude.

Being involved early in the development of something as significant as changing high schools nearly 30 years ago was both exciting and noteworthy; however, at some times, it was also a comedy of errors, because there was no history or preparatory guidelines at the time. My process was often "hit and miss": I found a theory that I thought would work; I believed it would work and trusted the process.

Hindsight, as usual, offers tremendous wisdom in channeling energy of passion and vision. With no preceding history, blind faith often superseded caution and judgment. As a result, many of the early reformers, including myself, made numerous errors that slowed the work and, in some cases, even created major blocks to the original redesign efforts.

Even though I am no longer in the principalship and am now teaching in a university principal preparation program, I frequently muse at the energy and effort expended in initiatives that are absolutely marvelous in theory but do not contribute as significantly as expected. It is interesting that current redesign initiatives still use many of the same processes in many of the same ways that we did as early reformers. Without planning and attention to research, schools are destined to re-create those interesting errors, although research and history remind us of their impact and potential to thwart sustaining power.

Now in a different place in my life and career, 20/20 hindsight and passion for high school redesign allow me the opportunity to offer suggestions to help energetic and enthusiastic practitioners nurture and sustain changes for school improvement.

Understanding and Nurturing the Work of School Improvement

Launching into the work of school improvement must be guided by a clear focus and an astute awareness of the issues that may substantially impact the results. Several issues must be understood to nurture the work of school improvement because of how they will shape sustaining the work.

1. Understanding the Difference Between Redesign or School Improvement and "Moving the Deck Chairs on the Titanic"

In the late 1970s and early 1980s, it was considered radical to shift the minutes in the class periods and in the day. Finding new configurations for courses was ground breaking because it flew in the face of the legislature and state statutory code. Finding ways to break large schools into smaller units so that teachers could know the students well, coupled with creating teams of teachers with an assigned team of students, was clearly cutting edge. Designing and moving schools into the block schedule was so innovative it was sure to shift emphasis to student-centered instruction. Renaming and reorganizing principals and counselors in an effort to support the new organizational structures was noted by an interested America.

There are a number of examples that can be classified as "moving the deck chairs." These are just a few, but they point out the planning and organization necessary to launch the many tasks that early reformers thought best typified implementation of student-centered reform work. When all was said and done, most of the structural and organizational changes equated to simply moving the deck chairs or "changing the fabric on the chairs" or "placing the chairs on another deck." The important, substantive changes necessary in the instructional delivery system were not touched in most cases. Change was endlessly discussed, and many interesting and effective strategies were introduced that clearly made a difference in the lives of many students; however, seldom was the work deepened throughout the entire school or sustained after the originating leadership left.

Lesson Learned: Most redesign and school improvement initiatives offer wonderful plans to create schools that move toward student-centered places of learning. Yet the heart and soul of these initiatives did not penetrate that sacred cathedral of faculty beliefs and practice. The impact is in the relationship between the teacher and the student. The remainder can many times just be window dressing.

2. Paying Attention to the Business of the Business

Many of the school improvement efforts guided teachers and principals through work that had wonderful intent (such as block scheduling) but were solutions for tonsillitis superimposed on cancer. Principals struggled with scheduling efforts to position academic teams with common conference periods in schools in which extracurricular activities were a strong community expectation. Conversations ensued that attempted to resolve needing the fourth period for varsity athletics, varsity band, French IV, Calculus II, or other singleton courses. Unable to resolve the conflicts, planning acquiesced, and the core teams originally designed to know the students better and meet their needs were compromised. Counselors were unable to place students into "pure" teams. Students crossed over into other teams to take certain courses.

A force supporting the compromise, in many instances, was the eager, available attention of school boards that thought the idea was plausible but in practice would not violate the constituency—teachers and parents—who often voted them into the position of trustee. Initiating principals were often helpless when influences from a higher level dictated what was to be done while unraveling much of the beginning initiative work. Principals were forced to begin damage control in an effort to maintain any of the work started.

Many of the structural changes (chairs moved) were completed, but most were superficial. Underlying the structural changes were the same problems plaguing the school before the school improvement effort. The business of the business pertains to the important struggle of shifting attention to a student-centered school from the traditions of the teacher-centered classroom. Focus on anything but those issues will severely impair redesign work.

Lessons Learned: Sustaining the work of school improvement is predicated on attention to the important work of student learning. The structural redesign of schools is truly an important matter if it is focused on increasing the possibility of learning, but if for any other reason than for the improved performance of students, the initiative will flounder.

3. Creating Understanding and Readiness for All Faculty

Several redesigners (DuFour & Eaker, 1998; Fullan, 2001; Sizer, 1992) have discussed the importance of bringing the faculty into the redesign movement. Even in the early days of the movement, principals included their faculty and even some parents and community members, but the plans were often developed without serious consideration of teacher training, which was absolutely mandatory for success of the intended project.

Exxon enabled the work of Ted Sizer's (1992) movement (the Coalition of Essential Schools) by funding change initiatives for 10 schools nationwide that included staff development programs. It was a wonderful idea, but the training was conducted at Brown University, which prohibited sending as many teachers as were necessary for the training. In addition, inspiring the vision was viewed as not as important as we understand that it is today. Some of the principals in the original movement believed that merely asking teachers and including them in the training was enough. As is evident in many "reformed" high schools today, that was not enough.

Unless the principal understands the importance of teacher development, provides support during implementation, and monitors the implementation appropriately, teachers will fade back to their original comfort zone. The tendency for many principals is to implement too many programs or initiatives that are disconnected, and sometimes contradictory, in too short a period of time. Consequently, the faculty members, in the heat of implementation, do not see the connection of their program with other department initiatives. Rather than see the big picture, they tend to maintain the isolation or become isolated on a particular team. This is especially true for elective or specialty teachers who are "assigned" to multiple teams or serve the entire school. These specialty teachers often find the original comfort zone much quicker due to the lack of connection to the change initiative, whatever that might be.

Suffice it to say, teacher development is extremely important. The greatest example of need for professional development throughout the country is that of instruction delivery for block scheduling. Many principals jumped on the bandwagon shortly after a number of schools began to see early "success." Teachers were drawn to the program because of the time offered for instruction and also for their conference periods. However, those of us early into the effort simply assumed that teachers would adjust and make efficient use of the time. Sadly, making that transition was not easy for many, and the valuable time seemed to mirror the regular 50-minute class period with extra time to do homework or classwork. For teachers who used this time wisely, students were able to make immense gains, with instruction orienting toward project-based learning and emphasizing student participation and interest.

Texas recently analyzed the state scores across the state to determine if students were doing better in schools with the block schedule than in those schools in which students were still in traditional scheduling. According to the results, the researchers could find no statistically significant difference between the two scheduling techniques. With this information and the massive funding losses, superintendents quickly moved schools back to the traditional schedule, which reduced the number of teachers and brought a common approach for all schools, particularly if there were multiple high schools in the district.

Lessons Learned: Do not assume that teachers and or administrators can or will make the transition without time to consider and examine the impact an initiative will have on them and their practice. Professional development is mandatory. Time for appropriate assimilation is even more important.

4. Providing Leadership for a Substantial School Improvement

It has fascinated me throughout the last 20 years as to why principals enter into the reform process for their school. In working with schools, the following reasons are evident either through covert admission or unconscious administration:

a. Generate funding for the school or district.

Interestingly, principals have applied for and received funds to assist in reform work for varied reasons. From my experience, there seems to be a continuum of reasons why principals make the effort to generate funding—everything from buying a program for the redesign to finding money to buy extra personal units.

b. Get personal advancement.

Eager to advance, this process was used by many individuals to gain attention for exemplary leadership to strengthen their resume and gain experience for future endeavors. Achieving early success is wonderful for the principal; however, it leaves the school void of leadership for the remaining parts of the initiative. As is evident from change performance in schools across the nation, such initiatives rely heavily on leadership.

c. Improve a school or district.

Many genuinely seek to improve a school. The money becomes a needed source of revenue to support the work. These principals' passion is evident in the investment of time and energy coupled with the altruistic motive to make the education world a better place.

d. Implement a theoretical framework.

There have been a number of individuals whose passion for improving instructional delivery has manifested in a theoretical design, namely, John Goodlad (1984), Ted Sizer (1992), and others. There are certainly others who have taken the step, but the intent is to pilot the theory and, if successful, scale the effort to expand to other schools across the country.

Following behind them are a number of vendors headed by individuals who have the dream of changing schools while creating a business and a revenue stream. These vendors often have a theoretical structure from which they work, but often cannot find the coaches and support personnel who can effectively lead redesign work in schools.

e. Blind understanding.

Unfortunately, some educators are so anxious to move forward that many have taken schools currently in the process of reform while having no notion of the process or of the traps that were in place due to a floundering implementation. Unless these principals are quick studies of the process, the momentum retreats while the individual is trying to understand what is happening to the school and to them. Historically, the new administrator not understanding the process tends to be the death knell for the implementation.

Lessons Learned: Leading a school improvement effort requires immense effort on the part of the principal intending the work. Many educators talk of what an administrator must possess or do to be successful in the effort. But in my experience, those who have been successful have

a. a clear notion of what their leadership skills are and are not. Their experience has taught them what skills and abilities will match particular schools better than others. This is critical to reform work;

b. an incredible ability to read the culture and climate of a school in an effort to find the mediators in the school, the teacher-leaders, and those drawing a paycheck. They clearly understand how to build a team and focus the faculty on the work;

c. a vision for school improvement that focuses on shifting the focus from a teacher-centered school to a student-centered school;

d. a wonderful sense of timing for implementation of certain portions of the school improvement initiatives;

e. work ethics and interpersonal skills that generate trust and build personal integrity with the faculty;

f. a sense of community that seeks and develops important partnerships in the school and in the community; and

g. a keen desire to know the students and keep their well-being first and foremost.

Obviously, all administrators will not possess all of these qualities, but those who have been successful demonstrate many of them. The important point is that the administrators must know themselves and develop considerable self-awareness of who they are and what they can do.

5. Communicating the Real Issues

Important in the continuing effort to improve is attention to communication. This is probably the most slighted leadership skill due to our own view of what is important to communicate and when to communicate it. Also shaping communication is what each stakeholder needs and desires from the communication process. If the administrator tends to be a person of few words, this could lead to a host of problems for all participants. If the administrator tends to provide unfocused verbiage that is not well considered, then the impact could be misleading and cause a number of unexpected problems. Consequently, it is important to carefully strategize the message, consider how it is to be delivered, and match the audience to whom it is to be delivered.

Lesson Learned: It is important to develop a plan for communication and follow through. It is also important to check with trusted friends to be sure that you are on target with your thoughts.

6. Identifying and Dealing With the Need for Change

Early reformers invested time working with their faculties to convince them that change was important. With the inbred thinking that "this is the way that we have always done it, so why do we need changes" pervading much of teachers' conversation, principals discovered that talking about the need for change was not as powerful as the belief system among the teachers. In addition, principals were plagued with the mantra that often emerged from teachers, "I was here when you came and I'll be here when you leave." These insidious pockets in the culture became small viral cells infecting the faculty, creating cultural illnesses from which many principals could never recover. Although some educators have provided suggestions to overcome some of these problems, in the policies regarding district teacher relations, removing these infectious pockets becomes almost impossible.

Lesson Learned: Identify the pockets of teachers who have philosophical differences and work to align their beliefs with the necessary changes in the building; however, quickly identify the point at which the teacher or staff member must be removed to save the momentum of the work.

Sustaining the Work

Sustaining best practices in school improvement is obviously much easier said than done. Theories abound, but for the most part, principals receive initial guidance and support but then are left to devise their own strategies to continue implementation and then deepen the work. Part of the initial strategies of many of the efforts deal with fee-for-service support at the beginning of the effort, but few offer the continued coaching without unaffordable fees to help principals through the murky waters. In addition, many of the vendors do not provide principals with coaches who have done this work or who even understand how to help the school move after it has deviated from the scripted coaching guide.

Considerations for Sustaining and Deepening the Work

Personally Acknowledge That the Effort Will Take a Minimum of Three to Five Years to See Any Lasting Improvement

Principals often begin the work and expect turnaround within 1 to 2 years after implementation. Realistically, it will take 3 to 5 years for substantial movement in an elementary school, 5 to 8 years for a middle school, and 10-plus years for a high school. The principal must be committed for the duration and understand that if the commitment is not present, do not make the effort.

Create a Plan That Is Well Designed, Well Coordinated, and Well Monitored

Under the pressure of needing to reform, many principals buy multiple programs, implement them all at the same time, and expect swift results. The design must be aligned in philosophy and coupled with professional development to promote a solid launch and long-term implementation. Purchasing the latest programs but failing to carefully weave them together will lead to disjointed instructional delivery and lack of faculty understanding. It is important that the faculty understand all of the pieces so that they too can verbalize the opportunities for the students.

Once under way, the principal must manage the coordination of the project, which includes reports back to the faculty, students, and parents. Coordination may be achieved through teacher-leaders, parent supporters, as well as administrators, but the final responsibility belongs to the principal; consequently, monitoring its progress and making adjustments when necessary is mandatory.

Understand That School Improvement
Is About People, Not Things

Reform takes place in the hearts and minds of people. To sustain organizational change, it must be paralleled with strict attention to enabling students and teachers to understand the change and assimilate the ideas necessary to move in the direction of the vision. Paying attention to the personal and emotional needs of faculty who begin this journey can be overwhelming and time consuming, but these are the essence of making it happen. Specific things to consider:

Work with the timid, the resistors, and the high fliers. Each will have issues to bring to the table that will require immense consideration and time. The principal cannot manage all of the required attention, so it is vital that well-designed strategies be put in place to assist each of the categories of faculty participants. The timid require patience and understanding of their issues with certain aspects of the work. The resistors require immense understanding as to why they are resisting. Often the reasons are legion and unfounded, but, occasionally, the reasons can be justified and a resistor recovered with plausible and supportive justification. Shove high fliers off the cliff with support and recognition.

Find the faculty mediators to clarify the message. In every faculty, there are teachers who serve as mediators for the principal's message. Although the entire faculty hears the principal's message, teachers with referent power mediate the message to their "audience." Managing their impact and sometimes the teacher is a formidable task that is often overlooked by most principals beginning redesign. These "hearings" occur in teachers' rooms, in the parking lot, in the hallway after school, or at the local bar or restaurant.

Work consistently with student groups. Remember that they can be influenced by teachers faster with immediate results. Students need to hear from the principal, not necessarily in large groups, but in intimate situations in which the passion and vision become infectious. The students must see that these changes are for their benefit, even at intermediate and middle levels.

Find the parents who become ambassadors. Parents will be a most positive force in recruitment and marketing; however, they too must understand the vision and the supporting reasons for the work and then be given legitimate responsibilities for which they can see the reward. Not managing this force can curtail effective change. Maneuvering through difficult areas such as athletics, band, and other traditionally difficult areas using supportive parents can certainly bridge the discussion to dialogue.

Identify and Nurture the Critical Mass

Due to the levels of commitment in any organization, development of a strong critical mass will create enough energy to draw the less-committed members of the faculty, while neutralizing portions of the nay-saying resistors. Nurturing faculty who make efforts toward the work affirms them that what they are doing is going in the right direction. While working in this nurturing environment, it is critical to be genuine and honest so that faculty quickly recognize your personal commitment to the work and your integrity.

Recognize Those Contributing to the Work

Whether teacher, student, parent, or administrator, recognize examples of work and contributions that extend the work. Teachers resist such acknowledgments, but the principal's acknowledgment of such work directs attention toward those things that exemplify the work. The recipient may be initially embarrassed about the recognition and may take kidding from the faculty, but that individual is clearly reinforced for the work and effort. There will be more to come from that individual, and he or she will be sought for advice by other faculty members.

Listen to What Is Not Said

Although this is an obvious statement, many principals only listen to the apparent words and fail to hear the message. Listening to what is not said is extremely difficult and requires the principal's full attention to the speaker followed by well-positioned questions that probe into the probable message. Such questioning allows the principal to bring out the real communication while affording the speaker dignity. It is important to not judge the speaker for not being forthcoming; just work to understand what is really being said. This process is time consuming but absolutely mandatory as the principal deals with each level of participant in the process.

Provide Professional Development

Effective professional development for any reform work cannot be done in the traditional six-hour sessions that are never followed up with feedback and constructive suggestions. In addition, the amount of professional development must be commensurate with what is reasonably expected of the teacher for that particular year of implementation. Asking teachers to implement several major projects that require multiple, parallel changes in what they do will contribute to project failure. Project-relevant professional development must be provided in small chunks accompanied by quality feedback and the process repeated over and over again. Instructional delivery professional development is more a change of heart and mental model than procedure.

Find a Trusted Confidant

Traversing this difficult journey is not without political traps, unrest, and bewilderment. Because the trees are much easier to view rather than the forest when in the midst of the work, it is imperative that a trusted confidant be identified with whom an objective picture can be drawn and the attributes of the work carefully discussed. This must be a person with whom difficult issues can be straightforwardly discussed, both personal and professional issues. When stuck, the confidant can be invaluable in identifying the blocks and assisting in developing more effective strategies.

Be Sensitive to Timing Issues

Often, the principal feels obligated to move the initiative quickly. In some instances, quick implementation may be the best thing to do. In most situations, however, there are critical periods that arise that enable the principal to implement features of the work more easily than others. The timing issues will be driven by an intuitive understanding of the faculty's momentum. If the principal does not generally recognize the appropriateness of timing, then conversations with another principal, trusted confidant, or an astute assistant principal could provide valuable input as to when the initiative needs to be moved further. In many cases, the adage, "timing is everything" is most appropriate.

In Summary

Principals play a profound role in creating effective schools. Based on my reflections of school improvement initiatives over 30 years of work with educators in reforming schools, identifying best practices is the beginning of creating successful schools. But effective principals have a vision for long-lasting reform; therefore, although identification is important, nurturing and sustaining these best practices are equally important.

SNAPSHOTS

Bus Driver Training

Lyman Goding
Plymouth, Massachusetts

We have had between 39 and 56 buses serving Plymouth Community Intermediate School for our 450 to 2,100 early teens. I personally believe driving a middle-school bus run is the most difficult of jobs because we do not employ monitors and, if you look at what is happening on the bus, you are not able to watch the road. I have volunteered to meet with and provide bus driver training to drivers on what works with teens, how to approach and prevent problems, and how to ask for support before dangerous things happen on buses. We also ask for and share drivers' successful strategies with each other on a "Try this, it works on my bus" information sheet.

Some of the bus driver suggestions include the following: Say "good morning" and "good-bye," take students aside if there is a problem instead of embarrassing them in front of their friends, follow through and remain consistent, assign seats by grade but let students pick a buddy to sit with, use the children's names when you speak to them, do not belittle students, talk to them as you would to another adult, and remember that most students want you to care. Other suggestions included: Listen to students, treat them fairly, explain what you expect, do not yell, pay attention, and have a good attitude.

Professional Development Guidelines

Andy Adams
Ava, Missouri

Be diverse with professional development. Do not get on one trend or accepted way of doing something. I believe teachers should be given several different ways to do things and that they should be allowed to adopt the way of their choosing that fits their particular teaching style.

Never let teachers go to a professional development workshop unless they make the commitment to teach a workshop and share the information with the remaining staff members once they get back to the school.

Two Tiers for Professional Development

Marla S. Brady
Boca Raton, Florida

Recognize that there are two tiers that need to be developed in a successful staff development plan. One gets developed to ensure that the whole school is on common ground with curriculum issues that are identified. The second tier is to recognize and honor the individual needs of professionals at their varying levels of professional growth. A quality professional development plan helps educators understand that their plan is part of their intellectual property right. The development that occurs has a value and becomes a part of their professional assets.

Book Studies

Melinda Reeves
Decatur, Texas

We have a yearly book study to broaden the teachers' knowledge of different ideas and subjects they may not have had exposure to or experience with. The most recent book studies have been with Ruby Payne's (1996) book *A Framework for Understanding Poverty*, so that all teachers could learn how to deal with people whose values are different than their own.

Then we did another book study on *Brain-Based Research* by Eric Jensen (2000) to change the school environment from a sterile place to a welcoming place where students and teachers wanted to be. As a result of this book study, we implemented having indirect lighting in the classrooms as well as playing soft music and waterfall sounds, and many classrooms have murals on the walls.

Summer Reading

Kathleen Haworth
North Hollywood, California

Good summer reading is reading all the articles you do not have time for during the school year in *Principal Magazine, Administrator,* and other educational journals. They give good insights and cover a lot of ground.

Summary

School Improvement Research: Involve faculty in accomplishing shared vision and a collaborative environment, recognize leadership at every level, acknowledge that all are accountable for student achievement, establish a culture of inquiry, individualize instruction, be open to new scheduling ideas, and continue learning.

Best Practices for School Improvement
From Award-Winning Secondary School Principals

- Collaborate for improvement
- Emphasize improved student learning
- Examine past practices
- Apply new knowledge
- Be open to modifying when needed
- Share evidence
- Implement mentoring programs
- Maintain direct contact with students
- Encourage differentiated instruction
- Provide effective and continual staff development
- Use data in making decisions
- Encourage lifelong learning
- Observe in the classrooms
- Improve academic rigor
- Stay focused on school
- Be patient in sustaining school improvement

SCHOOL IMPROVEMENT PLANS REFLECTION

1. In what ways do I support school improvement?

2. In what areas do I need to improve?

3. What are school improvement planning needs at our school?

4. What is the decision-making process at our school?

5. How do we use data in our decision-making process?

6. What are we doing on our campus to ensure that school improvements are sustained?

7. Which ideas in this chapter do I especially like?

8. How can we implement these ideas in our school?

9. How might they need to be revised to be successful on our campus?

ADDITIONAL RESOURCES

Breaking Ranks II
http://www.nwrel.org/scpd/sslc

Character Education
http://charactereducation.com

Coalition of Essential Schools
http://www.essentialschools.org

Data Works Educational Research
http://www.dataworks-ed.com

Harry Wong Tips Pages
http://www.harrywong.com

Middle School Pathways
http://www.pitsco-pathways.com

National Board Teacher Certification
http://www.nea.org

North Carolina Teaching Academy
http://21stcenturyschools.northcarolina.edu/center/index.html

Principal Magazine
http://www.naesp.org

Principals' Executive Program at the University of North Carolina,
Chapel Hill
http://www.ncpep.org/content.php/index.htm

School Administrator magazine
http://www.aasa.org/publications

Transition Program for Young Adults
http://www.nl.edu/academics/PACE

REFERENCES

Blaydes, J. (2003). *The educator's book of quotes.* Thousand Oaks, CA: Corwin Press.

Breaking ranks II. (2004). Reston, VA: National Association of Secondary School Principals.

Bushman, J., Goodman, G., Brown-Welty, S., & Dorn, S. (2001). California testing: How principals choose priorities. *Educational Leadership, 59*(1), 33–37.

Danielson, C. (1996). *Enhancing professional practice: A framework for teaching.* Alexandria, VA: Association of Supervision and Curriculum Development.

DuFour, R., & Eaker, R. (1998). *Professional learning communities at work: Best practices for enhancing student achievement.* Bloomington, IN: National Educational Service.

Fullan, M. (2001). *Leading in a culture of change.* San Francisco: Jossey-Bass.

Goodlad, J. (1984). *A place called school.* New York: McGraw Hill.

Harris, S. (2004). *BRAVO principal!* Larchmont, NY: Eye on Education.

Hunter, R. (2004). *Madeline Hunter's mastery teaching* (Rev. ed.). Thousand Oaks, CA: Corwin Press.

Jensen, E. (2000). *Brain-based research.* San Diego, CA: Brain Store.

Lambert, L. (2003). *Leadership capacity for lasting school improvement.* Alexandria, VA: Association for Supervision and Curriculum Development.

Payne, R. K. (1996). *A framework for understanding poverty.* Highlands, TX: Aha! Process.

Sizer, T. (1992). *Redesigning the American high school.* New York: Houghton Mifflin.

Southworth, G. (2005). Learning-centered leadership. In B. Davies (Ed.), *The essentials of school leadership* (pp. 75–92). Thousand Oaks, CA: Corwin Press.

CHAPTER SIX

Personalizing the Learning Environment for All

If you . . . take a fresh look at a child . . . you then become an
explorer with the goal of uncovering or helping your students
uncover the gifts and strengths that can nurture them as they
grow.

—*Herbert Kohl (1994, p. 79)*

In 1846, five-year-old Sarah Roberts walked with her father past five area
schools to reach her school. Sarah Roberts was black. More than 100 years
later, in 1950, eight-year-old Linda Brown walked with her sister through a
railroad yard to catch a bus to her school two miles from home. Linda Brown
was black. In 1968, the average schooling for Latino children in Texas was 4.7
years. Native American students were also virtually excluded from educational
opportunities (Mondale & Patton, 2001). In 2001, nearly all of America's
school-age children were enrolled in public schools, and we had "more people
under the roofs of public schools learning than in any of the advanced indus-
trial democracies," according to journalist Nicholas Lemann (as cited in
Mondale & Patton, 2001, p. 212). In fact, the U.S. Census Bureau reported on
August 11, 2005, that Texas had become the fourth state in which minority
groups make up more than half of the population, along with California, New
Mexico, and Hawaii (U.S. Census Bureau Public Information Office, 2005).

But the achievement gap still exists along racial lines.

Being culturally responsive to ethnic diversity is just one aspect of
what I call the "moral mosaic" that today's principal-leaders are challenged

173

to address. Our students come to us from homes of affluence and homes of poverty. Many have educated parents; many do not. Our students are male and female, and some are struggling with their sexual identity. Our students are recent immigrants; some are children of migrant workers. Our students learn in different ways. This is why Hodgkinson noted that "nothing is distributed evenly across the United States, not sex, race, religion, wealth, or educational level" (as cited in Owings & Kaplan, 2003, p. 5).

Our students come to school with a myriad of experiences that many times are completely dissimilar from the experiences of their teachers and principals. At the same time, the diversity of educators is becoming less and less. Although nearly 40% of U.S. students are nonwhite, only 14% of elementary teachers, 10% of secondary teachers, 16% of principals, and 4% of superintendents are nonwhite. Rather than "become mere technicians, administrative guardians, and nothing more than custodians of the institution" (Glanz, 2002, p. 90), courageous, committed principals are called to provide culturally responsive leadership for this diverse population of students and to creatively find ways to bridge the achievement gap.

To respond to the challenge to educate such a diverse population and meet the needs of all students, principals are challenged to personalize the learning environment in unique and creative ways. Among other things, this means that they must understand that there is a difference between equality and equity. Equality is about treating everyone the same; equity is about treating others in such a way as to meet their needs (Harris, 2005). Respecting that students have individual needs and providing work that is authentic is an important way that principals demonstrate their care for students, a key to academic success (Sergiovanni, 1992; Starratt, 2003). In addition, principals must communicate an expectation that everyone on campus is accountable for all children's learning (Scheurich & Skrla, 2003). At the same time, principals must support teachers in teaching and in understanding philosophies and methods that respect, value, and emphasize the strengths of students' experiences, home cultures, contexts, and languages. And all of this must happen in a welcoming environment.

In this chapter, award-winning principals share many of the best practices that are implemented on their campuses to personalize the school environment and support learning for all students. Heath Morrison leads his school in developing a vision statement that reflects what the school truly believes. Brent Curtice describes the importance of a welcoming environment, whereas Tommy Floyd reminds principals of what we need to know about our students. Sharon Toriello describes a building-based intervention team approach to early intervention and prevention. Other best practices include transition classes, working with low-performing schools, helping English-as-a-second-language (ESL) students, and many other ideas.

WHAT IS AND WHAT OUGHT TO BE

Heath Morrison
Waldorf, Maryland

One of the most important things that happened for our school occurred during my second year at Thomas Stone High School. As we planned for the upcoming year, we began our school improvement efforts by revisiting our vision statement. This process took quite some time because the staff felt it was important to have a vision statement that truly would say something about what we as a group of educators truly believed. As is the case with most schools, our vision statement began with, "We believe that all students can learn. . . . " The important change we made was to state, "And it is our responsibility to ensure that they do at high levels." This acceptance of responsibility for learning for all students is clearly in our vision statement. We have taken ownership and have a responsibility to ensure that we are not only bridging the achievement gap, but truly eliminating it.

We have defined the achievement gap at Thomas Stone High School as the difference between what is and what ought to be. What ought to be is that all students learn at high levels. What is, however, is that many minority students are performing below their peers. That gap clearly gives us the areas on which we need to work. To that end, we have redesigned our afterschool program for students who need the most assistance. We have created summer programs in which we identify students performing below grade level and provide intense math and reading remediation to ensure they are making the important transition between middle and high school successfully.

We have also adopted a philosophy that the diversity of our school will be reflected in all of our school programs. To that end, it is no longer acceptable to say that certain groups of students simply did not come out for an activity. We must be proactive rather than reactive to encourage them to participate. For example, although we are extremely proud that we have had a 300% increase in our students taking the challenge of advanced placement (AP) over the past four years, we are even more proud of the 400% increase in minority students.

A WELCOMING ENVIRONMENT

Brent Curtice
Paonia, Colorado

Although we may not be an ethnically diverse community, we are extremely culturally and socioeconomically diverse. At times, our populace appears to voice two completely opposite viewpoints, creating a much divided community. I have worked very diligently to keep politics out of our school and to merge these entities into one cohesive body. A segment of the population has chosen to attend the local alternative school, designed to help students who do not fit well into a traditional school curriculum.

My challenge has been to create a welcoming atmosphere at Paonia High School, allowing these nontraditional students to participate in extracurricular activities and to take courses not offered in their curriculum. This partnership has enabled us to help bridge the very real gap that exists in our community.

Another way that we have addressed the diversity in our population has been the implementation of the Career Action Plan program, whereby each student is assured of having an adult advocate on staff who acts as his or her advisor. This program allows us to treat each student as an individual with varying needs and interests and helps the student map a course of study that is best suited for his or her future. Knowing that there is someone special to whom each student can turn has created a more trusting and respectful atmosphere. The advisor-advisee partnership is one of the cornerstones of my belief that personal relationships are vital to build the kind of school I envision.

In any community, the school is important, but in a small, rural community, it is the focal point, and a positive relationship between the school and the community is vital. We have been fortunate to have outside experts who have been willing to supplement our curriculum with their time and expertise. Our Natural Resource class pairs each student to work with a professional in his or her field, whether it is a Division of Wildlife officer counting bighorn sheep or a fish hatchery employee who shocks fish to test for diseases. Using community resources in and out of the classroom has enriched our curriculum and has opened doors to a variety of professions.

What Every Principal Needs to Know About Students

Tommy Floyd
Somerset, Kentucky

Best practices for principals include knowing about your students. Here are some guidelines to follow:

- Student need comes before everything else. When you are finished as a principal, you will remember how you treated students. . . . They will remember how you treated them!
- Be fair more than correct: Never just let policy dictate a decision; get all the facts. That will be difficult with your pace.
- Never let the one be more important than the many. Never let that statement allow you to ignore the needs of the one!
- Look for ways to praise all of your students; find out what they do or want to do.
- Learn their names and something about them.
- Talk to them as though they were older unless they are acting much younger, and then never let them see you angry. You will be the only loser in the future when you deal with them again.
- Forgive seniors who made freshmen mistakes; kids grow up.
- Keep informed of any negative event (death of a loved one, fire, family divorce, etc.) that occurs in the life of a student. Be there for them, if only in a note or a brief conversation. This bears huge mileage.
- Showcase all individual successes.
- Find ways to put successful older students with unsuccessful younger students!
- Almost every student problem that students are dealing with is due to a lack of love somewhere. If you are brave enough, you can help them most of the time.
- Start a bulletin board and ask for their pictures. They will bring them, and when they return in the future, they will look for themselves.
- Never underestimate the power and effect that encouragement has on a young person who is still developing into who they will be!
- Do not give up on a single kid. Who will pick them up if not you?

BUILDING-BASED INTERVENTION TEAM

Sharon Toriello
Kinnelon, New Jersey

A building-based intervention team is a holistic approach to early intervention and prevention, in which a single committee deals with all aspects of students who are having problems. This is an extension of a core team concept that helps assist students and their families.

The intervention team meets once a week to discuss concerns that faculty have about specific students. All staff members can submit a referral on a student to the vice principal. Generally, the team has discussed the concern with the student and has contacted the guidance counselor and the parent prior to this. The vice principal consults with the guidance counselor and the student assistance counselor (SAC) to determine if there are matters of confidentiality regarding the student that would explain the behaviors of concern. If not, a checklist of behaviors is distributed to all the teachers of that student, the school nurse, and the school counselor. These are collected along with attendance and disciplinary referrals for behavior and are summarized by the SAC. This year, we e-mailed the form to faculty and staff and they return it, to speed up the process.

The student of concern is placed on the agenda of the weekly meeting, and results are then shared. The committee is made up of the SAC, the school counselors, the school nurse, a representative of the child study team (usually the school psychologist), two teacher representatives, and the vice principal. The data from the checklist include academic behaviors, attendance, disciplinary, and social and personal information. After reviewing the data, the team decides whether an intervention is warranted. If so, a plan is devised. If academics are concerned, a meeting is scheduled that includes all of the student's teachers and the guidance counselor. This committee meets with the student and parent, and a plan is devised to scaffold the student's academic performance, which could include tutoring by a teacher or peer, formalized communication with parents, or other strategies.

If problems are related to substance abuse, a meeting is arranged with the SAC, parent, student, and vice principal to review the checklists, express concerns about the reasons for the behaviors, and provide a list of outside resources, including providers for an assessment and treatment. The assessment is either recommended or required by board of education policy, depending on the severity of the behavioral problem. Parents are provided with written information about using insurance and approved providers who offer specialized services on a sliding scale for those who need financial assistance. The SAC follows up with the student and parent after the assessment and also during the treatment.

If the committee concludes that there are no strong concerns, the guidance counselor continues to monitor the situation. Referrals can also originate from the police department because our substance abuse policy requires those who are charged with any drug- or alcohol-related infraction to fall under the district policy. This means that these students undergo an assessment and follow the recommendations given. Many students in this category require some early intervention treatment that is educational for both student and family.

PROVIDING INDIVIDUAL ATTENTION FOR AT-RISK STUDENTS

Andy Adams
Ava, Missouri

We had great success with at-risk kids by having a teacher in each grade level of seventh and eighth teach six sections of at-risk science, math, and so forth. By doing this, these students received the individual care they needed. This also helped regular-education teachers in pacing their curriculum by not having to teach at two grade levels. I believe this system allowed the at-risk and regular classroom students to achieve at extremely high levels.

To make this work, we tried to keep the class sizes at about 12 to maximize the teachers' ability to make sure kids were getting the individual attention that they needed. We placed the students into this at-risk class through a couple of different methods. We filled out an at-risk checklist on all the kids at each grade level. We tried to keep them in the at-risk math and science, but placed them in the regular classroom for their other classes, provided they did not qualify for special classes in some other area. The teachers were aware of their situations, and we stressed the need to modify the curricula to make these kids successful. With the requirements of No Child Left Behind, kids need a continual learning process at their achievement level. We placed a teacher in these classrooms who possessed the attitude of a "true teacher," in that he or she believed that every student could learn and be successful. We were fortunate to have teachers who really believed in and cared for their students.

We enjoyed success with this classroom setting and increased our test scores. In addition, over the seven years I was principal, we sent kids to high school who were more successful. This resulted in the dropout rate of our high school being half of what it was a short time period before.

FRESHMEN TRANSITION PROGRAM— A BRIDGE TO HIGH SCHOOL

Sharon Toriello
Kinnelon, New Jersey

The freshman transition program at Kinnelon High School integrates several diverse activities that developmentally support the social and academic concerns students have as they move from middle to high school. We begin in February when students are eighth graders and continue through the end of their first semester as ninth graders to ease this transition. The calendar that we follow includes:

February	High school counselors meet with groups of middle school students at the eighth-grade parent evening program
March	High school counselors meet individually with eighth graders to plan their high school programs
April	High school exhibition and activities fair for eighth graders and their parents to view academic presentations in classrooms and meet representatives from all high school activities
June	Revisit eighth-grade teacher recommendations for ninth-grade placement. We assign students to read *The 7 Habits of Highly Effective Teens* and to complete a writing project
July	Schedule refinement
August	Freshman orientation
September	Freshman group activities/learning styles
Fall	Freshman orientation to guidance and counseling center
November	Peer interaction groups for low achievers
January	Strategies for review and exam preparation

Summer and Fall Transitional Activities

Many of these activities are based on *The 7 Habits of Highly Effective Teens*:

- *Activity 1:* Eighth-grade students are required to read *The 7 Habits* book during the summer before the ninth grade. They are asked to write a letter to themselves as if they were seniors, about to graduate, talking about their success in school. In this way, students visualize a successful high school experience, and habits connected with goal achievement are reinforced.
- *Activity 2:* Orientation Day—August. When freshmen arrive at school, they are met by upper-class "buddies." Activities include a one-hour workshop called "Making High School Count," a tour of the building following their schedules, and a pizza party.
- *Activity 3:* One month into the year, counselors do a follow-up orientation with a classroom presentation. This presents students with a proactive approach to learning in which they are encouraged to use and continually refine their habits to take responsibility for their successes and their setbacks.
- *Activity 4:* Freshmen are brought to the guidance office in small groups to continue enhancing their ability to visualize their successes, emphasizing the theme "beginning with the end." Activities include reviewing a typical senior's high school transcript and test record, discussing the impact of each quarter's grade on final grade point average, and beginning an electronic portfolio.
- *Activity 5:* In a continuing effort to more effectively work with underachieving students, those identified as experiencing academic difficulties based on progress reports meet with peer mentors to strategize ways to improve grades. Topics include goals, time management and organization, proactive ways to improve grades, getting involved in activities, and connecting today's efforts and tomorrow's choices.
- *Activity 6:* The final activity of the program takes place in January. Counselors meet with ninth graders in English classes to review study skills and learning styles. Topics include assessing previous success in studying for tests, using review materials to maximize exam grades, finding the "big picture," and using strategies for learning large amounts of material.

TRANSITION CLASS

Becke Cleaver
Winchester, Kentucky

At Conkwright Middle School, we have one class that we call a "transition class." Our superintendent wanted to downsize our alternative school, so he sent one teacher to each of two middle schools and one to the high school. I had to decide how best to use this teacher. I also disliked sending students to the alternative school. In Kentucky, alternative schools are not considered A1 schools, which means that state assessment scores do not get attached to the school. Instead, the alternative school reports to the state which school the students are supposed to be attending and the score goes there. The reason I did not like sending students is the school gets their scores, but gives up the control of what happens to them instructionally. Therefore we created this transition class.

If looping teams were having problems with a student, they could refer him or her to the transition classroom. We created a team including the assistant principal, the transition teacher, the team leader, a counselor, and so forth. Each team had two slots in the class and could send a child after approval from the team to the class. The student is assigned for nine weeks—one grading period. The student is in the class full time the first week, then he or she earns one class a week back starting with the student's strength area first. So if a child's best or favorite subject is math, he or she gets math class back the first week, and so on. At the end of the nine weeks, the student is back on his or her team.

The transition teacher works on behavior, continuing the same work from the team in the class supplemented by technology programs for additional support. If the child messes up, the transition teacher is called to remove him or her from class. The teachers can refer for any reason, such as behavior, failing grades, noncompletion of work, and conflict between other students. We cycled about 42 students through the program. We have eliminated alternative school and day treatment referrals altogether, and we are keeping our own students. It is a very effective program.

Strategies for a Low-Performing High School

Melinda Reeves
Decatur, Texas

When I started at Decatur High School nine years ago, it was labeled as a low-performing high school, and it had a very high dropout rate. The first thing that we did was address the dropout rate with a very progressive discipline and attendance system. We stayed on top of attendance by not excusing any absence unless the attendance clerk spoke directly with the parents by telephone.

We then addressed the academic issues by implementing specific reading strategies. We chose a program that I learned about through the National Association of Secondary School Principals called Reading Right. We wrote a grant and got the program for the school. This was a very powerful program, and we still use it today. It has even helped some of our Down syndrome students and our ESL kids.

We also created a summer camp in math and science for the at-risk students. We wanted to be able to form relationships with the kids and staff members. By building relationships, someone would know these students when they came to school, and that would create a sense of belonging.

We instituted a program called "Tuesday Extra." This means that the counseling office, the library, the computer lab, and some of the vocational programs stay open until 8:30 p.m. on Tuesdays. Next year, we will be expanding the Tuesday Extra program to include the social studies department and provide for tutors, and we will even provide bus transportation for students who do not have a way to get home.

To build and strengthen relationships with our students, we hold a "Fish Camp" for all incoming freshmen and their parents. The parents actually take off work and spend the day at the school. The parents learn about expectations and school procedures. The boys spend half of the day at camp and the girls spend the other half of the day, and then they come back together at night for the rest of the camp.

We started a SOAR program in which each teacher or administrator has a freshman advisory group that he or she meets with every other week of the students' freshman year. After the students' freshman year, they are still followed by their advisor, but not as closely. Faculty continue to check on their students throughout the four years they are in high school.

Implementing four different mentor programs has also helped us build relationships at Decatur High School. We have a student-to-student mentor program, a student-to-community mentor program, a student-to-teacher mentor program, and a teacher-to-teacher mentor program.

ESL Students and Reading

Evelyn Ennsmann
Villa Park, Illinois

At Willowbrook High School, we have a diverse population of students. Although the majority of our non-English-speaking students are Hispanic, we have many students who speak a wide range of approximately 30 other languages. Because we were concerned that our ESL students were not getting the help they needed in regular classes, we have created a special three-track reading/ESL emphasis for them. Beginning English speakers—ESL Level 1 students—participate in ESL learning three periods a day, in which only reading and language arts are emphasized. One is taught by a reading specialist; the other two periods are taught by an ESL teacher. Students are pretested at the beginning of the year, tested in midyear, and tested at the end of the year. As students move toward English proficiency, they are moved to ESL Level 2, to ESL Level 3, and then back into the mainstream for all of their class periods.

We have also created a literacy department, in which we have combined three separate services: reading, ESL, and instructional resources (tutoring). These were all independent programs, but by placing all of them under the same umbrella, we feel that all students will be served more effectively and there will be more uniformity in the school.

FIND AN ADVOCATE

Lyman Goding
Plymouth, Massachusetts

Here are five best practices for ESL and remediation strategies that we implemented:

1. Focus on finding an advocate for each ESL student. We pushed also to find a neighborhood adult leader who would support new immigrants. For example, a Brazilian store owner helped us with connections to his growing community and would come to school as an advocate with pride and expectations for kids in his neighborhood. We worked hard to get a parent school council representative from an affordable housing area so there was a connection.

2. Each new immigrant did an electronic portfolio in his or her home language and English so we could all get to know our new families.

3. Lunch menu signs as well as other information were written in multiple languages—food is what kids really care about!

4. We tried to locate and spend grant money, remediation, or No Child Left Behind money in neighborhoods if possible. Community centers in housing project areas are often very helpful if we provide the teacher; a great two-way connection was made to some potential hot spots.

5. We did buddy tutoring, encouraging a family member to come with the student to before or afterschool programs.

IMPROVING READING SKILLS

Dan Stepenosky
Beverly Hills, California

Students not achieving their identified learning potential or not meeting the school's performance standards receive special placements in the academic program. In the English department, students reading two or more years below grade level are placed in a developmental reading class where they receive a modification of the core curriculum. For example, all students read a Shakespeare play in Grades 9 through 12. Through vertical teaching methods, students in developmental English have more support, through a text with Shakespearean English on one side of the page and modern English on the other, a workbook with guided questions and activities, and more time devoted to the literature through additional teacher-designed activities. Students receive instruction in vocabulary and standard written English skills appropriate to advancing each student. They exit these specialized classes based on standardized test results, course grade, and teacher recommendation. Between ninth grade and eleventh grade, there is an average reduction of approximately 50% in the number of students in the developmental reading classes.

Individualized Graduation Plan

Tom Hamilton
Bardstown, Kentucky

Access to a rigorous curriculum is not only a goal at Bardstown High School but at all of our nation's secondary schools as well. Keeping that in mind, our mission here is to develop skills for greater performance and lifelong learning. One basic belief is that our role is to prepare students for education at the next level (whatever that may be).

We have developed an individualized graduation plan for each student entering Bardstown High School. Maintaining, updating, and monitoring that individual growth plan (IGP) is done through an advisor-advisee program. Each staff person, me included, maintains a relationship with a group of entering freshmen as they move through their high school career, and then we loop back to pick up another group as one group graduates. I am presently working with 17 sophomores whom I meet with on a regular basis. Early in the year we meet often—once a day for the first week—as we review their schedules and policies and procedures for the upcoming year. In late winter, the pace picks up again as students begin scheduling for the next year. The IGPs, which include data on transcripts, test scores goals, and extracurricular activities, are updated. For one meeting, the entire staff meets in the evening with their advisees so that parents can attend. As a matter of fact, our site-based council has required parents to personally meet with their student's advisor at least once per year. Needless to say, this has resulted in more than a few advisor-advisee conferences in the living room of many students' homes!

Data that measure the effectiveness of all our programs to personalize the learning environment are somewhat subjective. However, our dropout rate has dropped from 6.17 in 2001 to 2.31 in 2004. Our enrollment has increased from 360 in 1994 to more than 500 in 2004, with many of these students being tuition students who live in other districts. Our successful transition rate to college, work, or training programs has been 95% to 100% in the past five years. Our attendance rate has always run around 93% to 94% average daily attendance in a state that averages 87% to 88% for secondary schools.

Probably our best statistic is our community support. We have implemented a uniform policy and a drug-testing program for all athletes and extracurricular activities with both vocal and financial support. The trust between the school and the community is strongly evident.

DOUBLE PROMOTING STUDENTS

Marla McGhee
Austin, Texas

A review of campus data revealed a significant number of students who were over-age for grade level, especially in Grades 6 and 7. In collaboration with another administrator on campus (a progressive, student-centered colleague), I created a school within a school called the "Academy @ CD Fulkes." Using Title I funds, we developed an innovative accelerated program with the goal of double-promoting students by the end of middle school, allowing them to rejoin grade-level peers for their high school years of education. We carefully selected 60 of the most challenging-to-reach students as potential participants.

A series of conferences and information sessions were conducted with students and their parents to explain our plan and approach. We attracted three master teachers and three excellent instructional aides to work with academy students. Students' schedules were completely reconfigured, recapturing 300 instructional hours during the school year. Under the guidance of the instructional staff, students helped design rubrics for everything from academic performance to daily behavior. These sets of rubrics replaced traditional report cards for academy students. Technologies were used in an integrated fashion and infused across the curriculum. Students were also taken into the community for hands-on, real-world experiences, including daylong internships at local businesses. The results were quite remarkable. Numerous students who were at risk of dropping out due to multiple retentions stayed in school and eventually graduated as a function of participating in this program.

SNAPSHOTS

ACT Test Help

Evelyn Ennsmann
Villa Park, Illinois

The guidance office and media center provide practice ACTs and Pre–Standardized Aptitude Tests before school, during lunch, and after school for juniors who would like extra practice or who have test anxiety. Students use software to help them with skills they are lacking that particularly pertain to the ACT. They do not have to complete the entire test in one sitting but can go back when they have time. The practice test is timed and provides feedback to let students know how well they did and how long they took for each of the sections. Student feedback has been very high, and students are very pleased with the program because of the immediate feedback they receive. This is only one area in which they are given help.

Throughout the school year, we presented data from our program called "Explore, Plan and Act" to help parents and students see how their scores impact their choices of future schools they will be attending, as well as how their scores impact the school in meeting proficiency in the No Child Left Behind Act. These scores were also used to determine what types of interventions we provided for our students during lunch, before school during Monday late starts, and after school.

We provided our juniors with a test-taking strategy session to help them in test-taking situations. Our guidance staff and administration worked with students one on one to identify their areas of weakness and provide them with varied resources to help them with their skills. We also brought parents in to take portions of the ACT and use the software program so they could assist their students and be more aware of what was expected of the students. Parent sessions were provided at morning and evening sessions.

Strategies to Improve College Success

Melinda Reeves
Decatur, Texas

A major focus of our high school is to encourage kids to go to college. We have a sophomore plan to keep kids thinking toward their goals and to keep them on track for college. We conduct a senior retreat that includes the parents and tips for college, financial aid, and a senior survival guide for the senior year because there is so much to do and to keep up with during that year.

We have also made sure that our curriculum is horizontally and vertically aligned. By studying the research, we make sure that the curriculum is rigorous, which is the most important aspect of curricula. For example, when students take just one AP class, they have a 48% better chance of making it through college than those who have not had any AP classes.

Voluntary Student Mentor Program

Evelyn Ennsmann
Villa Park, Illinois

At Willowbrook High School, our juniors and seniors volunteer to mentor freshmen students. Juniors and seniors are assigned to a freshman study hall during their lunch hours two to three days a week to help freshmen in the areas of weakness. They help with homework, assist with projects, show them where their classes are, answer questions, and assist them in learning concepts that they may still not have totally understood. A teacher is assigned to each of the study halls as a facilitator for both the mentor and the mentee.

Although I began the mentor program by working with the principal-student leadership team, our guidance staff expanded the program and added a "New Beginnings" program for our freshmen as well. This provided support for them not only academically, but socially as well. The program was taken to a whole new level when two teacher-leaders in our guidance staff took over the program. Student mentors volunteered their time in the summer during lunch and after school for get-back-to-school meetings with their mentees. It is awesome!

A New Paradigm for Summer School

Marla McGhee
Austin, Texas

The traditional summer-school format was simply not working for our students. We began to specifically explore why students were not being successful in the regular classroom by canvassing each teacher of failing students. We examined homework and study practices as well as general understanding of the subject matter. Using this information, we fashioned an individual education plan for every student referred for summer school.

In addition, we approached summer-school instruction differently. Math and science, and history and language arts, were combined to create integrated, interdisciplinary courses. In addition, high-level instructional materials and lessons engaged students in active opportunities to participate and learn. We literally had to make students go home each day. They were so excited and engaged, they did not want to leave! The success rate for this approach to summer school was phenomenal.

Earlier Start to School

Marla McGhee
Austin, Texas

Because many C.D. Fulkes Middle School parents and guardians had jobs that required them to be on-site early in the mornings, it was not uncommon for students to arrive on campus more than an hour before the start of school. Because we were all there, we took advantage of it and initiated an earlier school start. Granted, we had to work through the details with the district transportation division as well as gain the endorsement of our site council and area assistant superintendent. But once we crossed those bridges, it was smooth sailing. Parents liked it, kids liked it, and teachers agreed, too, that it made good use of our day. It also helped to dramatically decrease the incidents of beforeschool behavior mishaps.

Diversity Is Our Strength

Tom Hamilton
Bardstown, Kentucky

We are one of three high schools in our community and the only one with a significantly diverse population. It has always been my belief that diversity is our strength, and we have publicly advertised that slogan. To meet the cultural and academic needs of all our students, we have made it the goal of the site-based decision team to integrate the curriculum with as many culturally diverse programs as possible throughout the year. Each year, we sponsor a lecture series patterned after a college program that exposes all of our students to diverse leaders in the community and state, many of them females or people of color who teach, engage, or simply entertain groups of students in small, intimate settings. We purposefully keep the group small to stay away from the "assembly-type" environment. Over the years, we have had government leaders, sports figures, movie producers, and educators who have chatted with and answered questions for our students.

Of course, we also have a big party on Martin Luther King Jr. Day each winter. Our Diversity Day celebration is famous throughout the community. In a program run entirely by students, both black and white, we sing, dance, read poetry, and produce skits that have resulted in standing room–only crowds in our auditorium at 10 o'clock in the morning. This program is in drastic contrast to programs we attempted (run entirely by adults) fewer than 10 years ago that resulted in tension, student protests, and community ambivalence.

Joining Forces

Dana Trevethan
Turlock, California

This past year, our English-learner (EL) population and at-risk students joined forces with our drama students, cheerleaders, and Spanish Club members to create, design, and participate in our state's Principal Lip Sync Contest—a contest geared toward providing Hispanic students with scholarship money based on competitive performances against other high school students in California. In previous years, our EL and Hispanic students had a difficult time finding success due to their lack of confidence and experience with organizing such performances. Because of this, we decided this past year to make every effort to assist our students by encouraging other student groups on campus to join forces and make the event a collective effort of student participation, motivation, and enthusiasm. As a result, our drama students, cheerleaders, and Spanish Club members took center stage with our EL and Hispanic students and myself (the principal) to earn first place in our region and fourth place at the state competition. More important than the final outcome was the experience of having students cross ethnic boundaries, erase social and economic barriers, and ignore clichés on campus to work together to achieve one common goal. Lasting friendships were built among students and staff this past year, and all stakeholders are looking forward to this year's competition and the continued building of relationships.

A Bus Ride Through the Attendance Zone

Marla McGhee
Austin, Texas

As I began to spend time at C.D. Fulkes Middle School, I felt, for many reasons, that some faculty members were not relating to our students. Numerous faculty and staff drove into the community each day to work then retreated to their own neighborhoods outside the C.D. Fulkes attendance area. To reconnect with our learners, we took a community field trip. On one of our professional development days early in the year, we secured several district school buses and placed on them sodas, snacks, a police officer, and a local realtor. We then piled onto the buses (similar to our students' daily experiences) and drove the entire attendance zone.

The police officer and realtor provided information and answered questions about neighborhoods as we drove through them. The C.D. Fulkes staff members remarked about attributes of the subdivisions and neighborhoods, noting there were not many open spaces or public parks for children to gather in or play. At the end of the experience, we were all much more aware of where our students were coming from each day when they arrived at school.

Safe Schools

Andy Adams
Alva, Missouri

Keep all doors locked coming into the building, except the one closest to the principal's office. As a rural school, one might never suspect we would have any problems. But I believe we were well advanced over most schools in the geographical area in that we never allowed anything to happen by being proactive in the protection of students. I even took a chain and truck and pulled all the trees and shrubs that were end to end in the back of the building. It would have been so easy for someone to have hidden in that growth. People in the town thought I was crazy for pulling all the trees and leaving the side of the building empty, but as they came to understand why I did it, the appreciation just grew.

Summary

Research on Personalizing the Environment: Create a warm environment, meet student needs, support high achievement for every student, acknowledge accountability for all, implement culturally responsive teaching strategies, and respect diversity.

Best Practices for Personalizing the Learning Environment From Award-Winning Secondary School Principals

- Celebrate diversity
- Acknowledge belief in students' learning capacity
- Commit to being responsible for all students
- Provide a welcoming environment
- Provide resources to help all students achieve
- Maintain high standards for all
- Support students in making transitions
- Support mentoring programs
- Advocate for students
- Support academics
- Build relationships with students
- Prepare students for future success
- Keep schools safe

PERSONALIZING THE LEARNING ENVIRONMENT FOR ALL REFLECTION

1. How diverse is our student population?

2. How diverse is our faculty?

3. What are the needs of our at-risk students that are being addressed effectively?

4. What are the needs of our at-risk students that are not yet being addressed?

5. What kinds of relationships do I build with my students?

6. Which ideas in this chapter do I like?

7. Which ideas would I like to know more about?

8. How can we implement new ideas in our school?

9. How might new ideas need to be revised to be successful on our campus?

ADDITIONAL RESOURCES

ACT
http://www.actstudent.org

Career Action Plan Program
http://www.jobweb.com/Resources/Library/Career_Pursuit/Career_
Action_Plan_103_01.htm

Explore, Plan and Act
http://testdev.act.org/explore/tests/epas.html

Reading Right
http://www.readright.com

REFERENCES

Glanz, J. (2002). *Finding your leadership style*. Alexandria, VA: Association of Supervision and Curriculum Development.

Harris, S. (2005). *BRAVO teachers! Building relationships with actions that value others*. Larchmont, NY: Eye on Education.

Kohl, H. (1994). *I won't learn from you.* New York: New Press.

Mondale, S., & Patton, S. B. (Eds.). (2001). *School: The story of American public education.* Boston: Beacon Press.

Owings, W. A., & Kaplan, L. S. (Eds.). (2003). *Best practices, best thinking and emerging issues in school leadership.* Thousand Oaks, CA: Corwin Press.

Scheurich, J., & Skrla, L. (2003). *Leadership for equity and excellence.* Thousand Oaks, CA: Corwin Press.

Sergiovanni, T. (1992). *Moral leadership.* San Francisco: Jossey-Bass.

Starratt, J. R. (2003, November 15). *Responsibility, authenticity, and presence: Educational virtues for educational leaders.* Speech presented to Phi Delta Kappa meeting at Stephen F. Austin State University, Nacogdoches, TX.

U.S. Census Bureau Public Information Office. (2005, August 11). *Texas becomes nation's newest "majority-minority" state, Census Bureau announces.* Retrieved April 6, 2006, from http://www.census.gov/Press-Release/www/releases/archives/population/005514.html

CHAPTER SEVEN

Words of Wisdom

> Advice is like the snow. The softer it falls, the deeper it sinks
> into the mind.
>
> *—Samuel Taylor Coleridge (as cited in Blaydes, 2003, p. 91)*

Famous quotes are great ways to motivate and inspire ourselves and others. Most of us have a favorite famous phrase in our office, on our desk, or carefully folded away in our billfold. Sometimes, we say these things so often that they become associated with us. A principal friend of mine used the saying "This too shall pass" every time things got difficult. Even now, years later, I cannot think of her without hearing that phrase in my mind.

When I asked award-winning principals to share their best advice, I did not expect the wide variety of words of wisdom they would share. I expected there to be some duplication of wise sayings, but none were the same. Instead, they shared words of wisdom that ranged from always keeping kids first to encouraging others to be risk takers, and all are guidelines for effective professional and personal growth. I hope these brief nuggets of wisdom and advice from fellow principals will inspire and motivate you.

> Think before you do—what bad can come out of your actions
> and what good can come from them?
>
> *—Andy Adams*

I don't often repeat the same statements, though I am fond of using cartoons from the daily paper to emphasize where we are

197

at a certain time and allow us to laugh at ourselves. Laughter is a healer and a motivator, and a good sense of humor can get us through tough times.

—*Sheila Anderson*

Autograph your work with excellence!

—*Diane Baker*

Don't let any program or policy be on autopilot. When you stop paying attention, I can guarantee that it will definitely veer off the road.

—*Stan Beiner*

The kids come first.

—*Stan Beiner*

Parents are our partners. They know their kids better than we do.

—*Stan Beiner*

Nurture your faith, family, and friends, and allow these three to do the same for you.

—*Tim Brady*

We as a staff will always do what's best for kids.

—*Stewart Carey*

Don't take the monkey! Everyone approaches you with a problem they want you to take. The challenge is can you support them, deal with the problem (the monkey), and let them keep it? It is a unique way to learn to delegate and maintain a smile on your face (thinking about a monkey sitting on the shoulders of the teacher standing before you!).

—*Becke Cleaver*

It's all good!

—*Brent Curtice*

Never settle for less than your best.

—*Susan G. Curtis*

Treat students the way you would want to be treated, and believe in every one of them.

—Evelyn Ennsmann

All students can learn. All students will be able to learn when they know that there is an adult in the building who cares about them and who they know they can count on.

—Evelyn Ennsmann

Bottom line on decisions: the best interests of kids.

—Anthony Ferreira

Your number one job as a principal is to put the most highly trained, highly motivated teachers in front of the kids *every* period of the day. All other jobs become easy if you accomplish number one.

—Kevin Fillgrove

Teachers have the most important job in the world, but I have the best, because I get to be a part of all the great things that go on at this school.

—Kevin R. Fitzgerald

Children and their needs must come first.

—Tommy Floyd

There is never enough love in the world.

—Tommy Floyd

For these are all our children . . . we will profit by, or pay for, whatever they become.

—from James Baldwin, and
often quoted by Dorothy Garrison-Wade

Establish high expectations and standards for all students and they will meet the challenge.

—Dorothy Garrison-Wade

Where good things happen every day. (I used this a few times, but it stuck as a school motto.)

—Lyman Goding

We're all doing the best we can; we will do better or differently with new and better information, and that is my job/our job— to provide new information. (This is based on a William Glaser idea.)

—*Lyman Goding*

This is important. You can do it. We are not going to give up on you—even if you give up on yourself. (These are phrases from John Saphier's book *The Skillful Teacher*.)

—*Lyman Goding*

Reserve judgment until all the facts are on the table, and take nothing for granted.

—*Eric Grantz*

I love my job!

—*Tom Hamilton*

Always make lemonade out of lemons. Translated for schools, in every situation, you can turn a volatile parent into an ally— just apply some effective listening and look for the shades of gray.

—*Kathleen Haworth*

Children first: You make a difference.

—*Carole Hiltman*

Make it a great day or not; the choice is yours. (This is said every morning as part of our announcements. It is fun to hear the kids and adults use the phrase as well during the course of the school day because it does catch on and becomes a great teaching/learning phrase.)

—*Marla S. Brady*

Everyone has something critical to contribute to our learning community.

—*Marla McGhee*

Meet our students where they are and take them where they need to be.

—Heath Morrison

Focus on the three Ps—professional, proactive, passionate—not perfect.

—Heath Morrison

It doesn't matter what you say—it's what you do that really matters.

—Allan Mucerino

Don't be afraid to try something new. When you implement something new, you have to do continuous evaluation of the program; know that the program will not be perfect. Change or improve as needed, stay on top of the research, use the research, look at your data and know where you need to grow and change, do not be afraid to take a risk.

—Melinda Reeves

Treat all kids the way you want your own child treated.

—Melinda Reeves

Let's think outside the box.

—Melinda Reeves

Discipline and love go hand in hand.

—Melinda Reeves

We need to reach consensus.

—Melinda Reeves

There is a creative solution to this problem.

—Melinda Reeves

Don't rest on your laurels.

—Mark Roherty

Be ready to take the heat when you say no.

—Mark Roherty

All students can learn—not necessarily in the same way and on the same day, but learn they can!

—Manette Schaller

Learning must always be at the center of what we do.

—Manette Schaller

Lead by example.

—Manette Schaller

To have balance in your life, get a subscription to *O Magazine*.

—Manette Schaller

People don't care how much you know, until they know how much you care.

—Kristine Servais

It's all about relationships and team building.

—Dan Stepenosky

Never say no when you can say yes.

—Marilyn Svaluto

When making decisions, always ask: Is this best for this child? and What would I want for my own child?

—Marilyn Svaluto

Let's talk through this as a team. There is nothing we can't resolve.

—Sharon Toriello

If they're not someone I would feel comfortable having as my own child's teacher, they're not good enough for any of my students. (This is the premise on which I hire and retain teachers.)

—Dana Trevethan

It's never too late to be what you might have been.

—George Eliot (James Wells)

WORDS OF WISDOM REFLECTION

1. What words of wisdom guide my professional practice?

2. What words of wisdom guide my personal practice?

3. What words of wisdom listed here would be most helpful for me?

4. What can I do to incorporate these truths in my personal and professional life?

REFERENCE

Blaydes, J. (2003). *The educator's book of quotes*. Thousand Oaks, CA: Corwin Press.

CHAPTER EIGHT

Recommended Reading List

We must form our minds by reading deep rather than wide.
—*Marcus Fabius Quintilian*
(http://www.brainyquotes.com)

I asked principals to tell us what books they considered to be "must reads" that help principals be more effective. Some of the books were suggested by more than one person, so I compiled all of the books into one list. Certainly, this list does not include all of the great books that have been written that contributed to principals becoming successful, but it is a great place to start the quest.

Atwell, N. (1989). *In the middle: Writing, reading, and learning with adolescents.* Portsmouth, NH: Heinemann-Boynton/Cook.
Barth, R. (1990). *Improving schools from within.* San Francisco: Jossey-Bass.
Barth, R. (2003). *Lessons learned: Shaping relationships and the culture of the workplace.* Thousand Oaks, CA: Corwin Press.
Barth, R. (2004). *Learning by heart.* San Francisco: Jossey-Bass.
benShea, N. (2000). *What every principal would like to say.* Thousand Oaks, CA: Corwin Press.
Blankstein, A. (2004). *Failure is not an option: Six principles that guide student achievement in high-performing schools.* Thousand Oaks, CA: Corwin Press.
Buckingham, M., & Coffman, C. (1999). *First, break all the rules: What the world's greatest managers do differently.* New York: Simon & Schuster.
Collins, J. (2001). *Good to great.* New York: Harper Collins.
Corwin, M. (2000). *And still we rise.* New York: William Morrow.

Costa, M. (2000). *Habits of mind*. Alexandria, VA: Association of Supervision and Curriculum Development.

Covey, S. (1989). *The 7 habits of highly effective people: Powerful lessons in personal change*. New York: Simon & Schuster.

Cunningham, P., & Allington, R. (2002). *Classrooms that work: They can all read and write* (3rd ed.). New Jersey: Pearson P T R.

De Saint-Exupery, A. (2000). *The little prince* (R. Howard, Trans.). New York: Harcourt.

DuFour, R., & Eaker, R. (1998). *Professional learning communities at work: Best practices for enhancing student achievement*. Bloomington, IN: National Education Service.

DuFour, R., Eaker, R., & Karhanek, G. (Eds.). (2004). *Professional learning communities: How professional learning communities respond when kids don't learn*. Bloomington, IN: National Education Service.

Evans, R. (1996). *The human side of school change*. San Francisco: Jossey-Bass.

Fullan, M. (1997). *What's worth fighting for in the principalship?* (2nd ed.). New York: Teachers College Press.

Fullan, M. (2003). *The moral imperative of school leadership*. Thousand Oaks, CA: Corwin Press.

Garmston, R., & Wellman, B. (1999). *The adaptive school*. Norwood, MA: Christopher-Gordon.

Gladwell, M. (2005). *Blink: The power of thinking without thinking*. New York: Little, Brown.

Goodman, E. (1979). *Turning points: How people change through crisis and commitment*. Garden City, NY: Doubleday.

Hall, G., & Hord, S. (2000). *Implementing change: Patterns, principles, and potholes* (2nd ed.). Boston: Allyn & Bacon.

Harris, S. (2004). *BRAVO principal!* Larchmont, NY: Eye on Education.

Heidner, J. (2005). *The Tao of leadership*. Atlanta, GA: Humanics.

Jackson, A.W., & Davis, G. A. (2000). *Turning points 2000*. New York: Carnegie Corporation.

Jensen, E. (2000). *Brain-based learning* (Rev. ed.). San Diego, CA: Brain Store.

Johnson, S. (1998). *Who moved my cheese?* New York: G. P. Putnam & Sons.

Kennedy, J. F. (1956). *Profiles in courage*. New York: Harper & Brothers.

Kohl, H. (1995). *I won't learn from you: And other thoughts on creative maladjustment*. New York: New Press.

Kotter, J. (1996). *Leading change*. Watertown, MA: Harvard Business School.

Kouzes, J., & Posner, B. (2003). *The leadership challenge*. New York: Wiley, John & Sons.

Krzyzewski, M. (2001). *Leading with heart: Coach K's successful strategies for basketball, business, and life*. New York: Warner Books.

Lee, B. (1998). *The power principle: Influence with honor*. New York: Simon & Schuster.

Leff, J., Smith, J., & Hines, E. (1999). *Making skill standards work: Highlights from the field.* Newton, MA: Education Development Center.

Marzano, R., Pickering, D., & Pollock, J. (2001). *Classroom instruction that works: Research-based strategies for increasing student achievement.* Alexandria, VA: Association for Supervision and Curriculum Development.

Maxwell, J. (1998). *21 irrefutable laws of leadership: Follow them and people will follow you.* Nashville, TN: Thomas Nelson.

Maxwell, J. (2003). *The 17 indisputable laws of teamwork.* Nashville, TN: Thomas Nelson.

McCarney, S. B. (1988). *The pre-referral intervention manual.* Columbia, MO: Hawthorne Educational Services.

McIntosh, G., & Rima, S. D. (1997). *Overcoming the dark side of leadership.* Grand Rapids, MI: Baker.

Morris, A. M. (1995). *The new leaders: Leadership diversity in America.* San Francisco: Jossey-Bass.

National Association of Secondary School Principals. (1996). *Breaking ranks: Changing an American institution.* Reston, VA: Author.

National Association of Secondary School Principals. (2004). *Breaking ranks II: Strategies for leading high school reform.* Reston, VA: Author.

National Middle School Association. (2003). *This we believe.* Waterville, OH: Author.

Ouchi, W. (2003). *Making schools work: A revolutionary plan to get your children the education they need.* New York: Simon & Schuster.

Payne, R. (1996). *A framework for understanding poverty.* Highlands, TX: Aha! Process.

Payne, R. (1998). *Working with students from poverty.* Highlands, TX: Aha! Process.

Ramsey, R. D. (2005). *Lead, follow, or get out of the way: How to be a more effective leader in today's schools* (2nd ed.). Thousand Oaks, CA: Corwin Press.

Roberts, W. (1990). *Leadership secrets of Attila the Hun.* New York: Warner Books.

Rogers, S., Ludington, J., & Graham, S. (1999). *Motivation and learning* (3rd ed.). Evergreen, CO: Peak Learning Systems.

Ross, J. (1966). *This we believe: Meditations on the Apostles' Creed.* Nashville, TN: Abingdon Press.

Rutherford, P. (1998). *Instruction for all students.* Alexandria, VA: Just Ask.

Senge, P. (2000). *Schools that learn.* Mechanicsburg, PA: Doubleday.

Sergiovanni, T. (1996). *Moral leadership: Getting to the heart of school improvement.* San Francisco: Jossey-Bass.

Sergiovanni, T. (2007). *Rethinking leadership: A collection of articles* (2nd ed.). Thousand Oaks, CA: Corwin Press.

Sims, P. (1996). *Awakening brilliance: How to inspire children to become successful learners.* Brampton, Canada: Bayhampton.

Thorpe, R. D., Jr. (1995). *The first year as principal: Real world stories from America's principals.* Portsmouth, NH: Heinemann.

Tomlinson, C. A., & Allan, S. D. (2000). *Leadership for differentiating schools and classrooms.* Alexandria, VA: Association for Supervision and Curriculum Development.

Wheatley, M. (1999). *Leadership and the new science: Discovering order in a chaotic world* (Rev. ed.). San Francisco: Berrett-Koehler.

Whitaker, T. (2003). *What great principals do differently.* Larchmont, NY: Eye on Education.

Wong, H. K., & Wong, R. T. (2004). *The first days of school: How to be an effective teacher.* Mountainview, CA: Harry K. Wong.

Zemelman, S., Daniels, H., & Hyde, A. (2005). *Best practice: Today's standards for teaching and learning in America's schools* (3rd ed.). Portsmouth, NH: Heinemann.

RECOMMENDED READING LIST REFLECTION

1. Of the recommended books, which ones have I already read?

2. Of the recommended books, which ones do I want to read?

3. What books have I read that I think are a must for effective principals to read?

CHAPTER NINE

Conclusion

Though no one can go back and make a brand new start,
anyone can start from now and make a brand new end.
                            —*Carl Bard (as cited in Blaydes, 2003, p. 92)*

Don't keep forever on the public road, going only where others
have gone. Leave the beaten track occasionally and drive into
the woods. You will be certain to find something you have
never seen before.
                    —*Alexander Graham Bell (as cited in Blaydes, 2003, p. 145)*

For nearly three years, I have been working on some aspect of the best practices of award-winning principals project. At one point, I even began calling it the "never-ending project!" Every day, I would scan my computer eagerly to see what successful practices a principal had submitted. I had the same feeling of anticipation at the mailbox or when the telephone would ring. For example, even now, months later, I remember with pleasure my telephone conversation with Principal Lyman Goding, whom I had never met, but the richness of our discussion as he shared his best practices still lingers. I saved the note I received from Melinda Reeves, who with her book submission, commented, "We have some really cool projects we're putting in place this year. You should follow up!"

In the introduction letter that I sent to hundreds of award-winning principals across the nation, I suggested at least 12 different topics that included standards, accountability, diversity, parent programs, and others. But when I read the more than 100 best practices that were submitted for this book from 34 award-winning principals, I was not surprised to see how consistent they were with the research on effective schools. The correlates of effective schools are defined as

- a clear school mission;
- high expectations for success;
- effective instructional leadership and practices;
- frequent monitoring of student progress;
- the opportunity to learn and using time for instructional purposes;
- ongoing curriculum improvement;
- a safe, orderly, and positive environment; and
- support of home-school relations (Lezotte, n.d.; Taylor, Pearson, Peterson, & Rodriguez, 2002).

Within the last few years, findings from several large-scale research studies reported in Taylor et al. (2002) have enhanced this list to include

- putting students first to improve student learning,
- strong building leadership,
- strong teacher collaboration,
- a focus on professional development and innovation,
- consistent use of student performance data to improve learning, and
- strong links to parents.

As I read through the principals' submissions, six themes began to emerge, all of which emphasized different leadership aspects of the principal's job and all of which connected with the effective schools research. The content of the best practices submitted by participating award-winning principals suggests that secondary school principals who lead effective schools emphasize the following best practices, all of which are consistent with research:

- Strengthen leadership to set direction, develop people, and redesign the organization.
- Shape and define a positive campus culture.
- Communicate to collaborate effectively with teachers, students, parents, and the larger school community.
- Encourage and oversee authentic curriculum and instruction for all students.

- Implement student- and learning-centered school improvement strategies.
- Personalize the learning environment for all students.

Secondary principals spend nearly 80 hours each week working on their campuses or attending school-related events. In this time frame, their best practices are characterized by implementing these six components of the principal's job by leading, mentoring, modeling, collaborating, visioning, communicating, learning, being accountable, collecting data, politicking, finding resources, investigating, leading staff development, supervising, and so much more. In the process, their best practices are a strong reflection of solid, research-based practices.

In addition, just as I had noticed with the elementary principals' best practice submissions, the same three themes resonated at some point in nearly every secondary principal's response: (a) we, not me; (b) people, not programs; and (c) students, not schools:

- Effective schools are built when *we* work together.
- *People*, not programs, make schools successful.
- Education is about *students*, not about schools.

WE, NOT ME

When principals talked of their best practices, they rarely talked about what "they" did. Instead, they commented over and over about what "we" are doing on "our" campus. For example, Sheila P. Anderson noted that "we know where we are going: all children successful." Tim Brady pointed out that "any success that I have had in school leadership is credited to what others formally or informally shared." Brent Curtice recognized that the school bond issue was passed because "we" worked together. Stan Beiner, in describing what his school did to gather feedback from community members, used the word "we" or "us" seven times in one short paragraph.

Marla McGhee recognized the "terrific assistant principals" who strengthened her leadership. Tommy Floyd reminded us that superintendents are part of this effective school team. Heath Morrison credited "the request of parents" for establishing weekend sessions to better prepare students for college. When Evelyn Ennsmann wrote about the great things happening on her campus, she was careful to give credit to various staff members by name. In addition, Eric Grantz told about "engaging our entire school community" in an effort to develop a collective vision.

In acknowledging this shared responsibility for school improvement at all levels, Anthony Ferreira noted the importance of building trust at all levels, whereas Manette Schaller commented on the importance that "we have a sense of humor." Kathleen Haworth likened this to "everyone . . . in the boat rowing in the same direction." Dan Stepenosky identified the importance of working with collaborative groups of other educators as essential to best practices. Successful principals understand the importance of collaborating and working with others. They appreciate the notion of a community of learners, and they encourage and welcome faculty, students, parents, and community stakeholders to be part of the team. They know the power of "we, not me."

PEOPLE, NOT PROGRAMS

Programs have one primary purpose in schools: to provide hope for everyone. When Tommy Floyd wrote about the demands of the principal position, he emphasized that this is a "place where *you* can make a real difference for kids." His best practice emphasis was on what principals can do for the people in the school, not on the programs. Heath Morrison, in addressing the challenge of the position, noted the "need for excellent people" rather than emphasizing the need for programs. And in that same vein, Kevin Fillgrove reminded us of the importance of surrounding oneself with others and benefiting from their strengths. Throughout Marilyn Svaluto's description of her detention hall program that involved walking, she identified ways that students were helped. Sharon Toriello shared "our" best practice of theme-based education, which this past year was all about commitment—commitment to students and their success.

Carole Hiltman pointed out that her students made dramatic increases in achievement not because of "a particular instruction technique or reading program" but because the people—students, parents, and staff members—took responsibility for increasing student progress. Likewise, Dana Trevethan's school created a student academic achievement plan with the intent to "provide our underperforming students" with extensive academic counseling. In writing about his school's looping program, Kevin Fitzgerald emphasized, "This allows the students to feel like members of a smaller learning community rather than just being 'a face in the crowd.'" Becke Cleaver tied the success of looping to accountability because "I can't afford to have a student with a marginal teacher." Marla S. Brady reminded us that when students "enter the school reading below grade level, we have to take them where they are and push them to their potential." When Lyman

Goding and Eric Grantz shared about their community service programs, both emphasized the benefit to the community, as well as to the students who participate.

Diane Baker noted the difficulty of the principal's job because it carries so much responsibility, "plus you are dealing with people, which means relationships." Brent Curtice challenged principals to build strong relationships with students and also with staff members. How people are treated is a best practice that guided Susan Curtis's leadership. Andy Adams echoed a similar challenge when he emphasized that everyone should be treated the way "you would want to be treated." Melinda Reeves's school held a "Fish Camp" and created a special program called SOAR to strengthen relationships with students in the high school.

Award-winning secondary school principals understand that people are the most important resource at the school. It is people who administer the programs. Programs are a vehicle with one primary purpose, and that purpose is to facilitate student learning. Schools are about people, not programs.

STUDENTS, NOT SCHOOLS

When all of these secondary principals talked about best practices at their schools, invariably, they noted that everything they did was focused on students and their achievement. For example, Manette Schaller asked, "What is it we want all students to learn?" Brent Curtice reminded us of the challenges that "our students face [in] a constantly evolving world." Dan Stepenosky pointed out that at his school, everyone is "aggressively committed to the idea that meeting the needs of every child is our guarantee of a better tomorrow for the entire community." Allan Mucerino challenged educators to build curriculum to fit the needs of students.

Emphasizing the importance of students is so critical Tommy Floyd wrote that "faculty and staff will not follow your lead . . . if they think you are not there for the kids first!" Tom Hamilton said that his school has a motto that focuses all of the decision process on one priority, "Do what is best for kids." Kristine Servais referred to this as student-centered leadership and always asked the question: "How is this good for kids?" James Wells pointed out in an e-mail to me that "high school kids are really children in big bodies . . . I try to do many things to stay connected to the kids."

Dorothy Garrison-Wade reminded us that important best practices are those that acknowledge that everyone on the campus is a potential student and "together, we open new doors and explore uncharted ideas" on our way toward self-actualization. Stewart Carey completed his submission by noting that at his school, "we are committed to leaving no child behind." Award-winning secondary principals were very clear that education is about students, not schools.

A Force for Good

I began this book by talking about the tremendous challenges of being a principal in the 21st century. I noted that although the media may be busy decrying school failure, there are many wonderful things happening on our school campuses. In each chapter, award-winning principals have shared their best practices, their successes, and their good news. But focusing on our strengths and sharing what is working does not mean that principals can or will forget the failures. Instead, they will be better equipped to turn those failures into successes because the very act of encouraging other principals with good news rekindles the spirit.

Thirty years ago, Robert Greenleaf (1977), in his classic book *Servant Leadership*, told about one of his old professors who complained that we were becoming a nation dominated by large institutions—churches, businesses, governments, labor unions, universities. The old professor complained that these institutions were not serving our needs well. He then challenged his students to be concerned about this by saying,

> Now you can do as I do, stand outside and criticize, bring pressure if you can, write and argue about it. All of this may do some good. But nothing of substance will happen unless there are people inside these institutions who are able to (and want to) lead them into better performance for the public good. Some of you ought to make careers inside these big institutions and *become a force for good—from the inside*. (Greenleaf, 1977, pp. 15–16, emphasis added)

In the difficult circumstances of education in this 21st century, when leaders are as likely to bear the brunt of blame as to be recognized for their award-winning work, secondary school principals are challenged to continue to lead our schools with best practices. They have become a force for good from the inside. Helping all students learn remains their passion.

References

Blaydes, J. (2003). *The educator's book of quotes.* Thousand Oaks, CA: Corwin Press.

Greenleaf, R. K. (1977). *Servant leadership.* New York: Paulist Press.

Lezotte, L. W. (n.d.). *Revolutionary and evolutionary: The effective schools movement.* Retrieved October 11, 2005, from http://www.effectiveschools.com/

Taylor, B. M., Pearson, P. D., Peterson, D., & Rodriguez, M. C. (2002). *The CIERA school change project: Supporting schools as they implement home-grown reading reform.* Retrieved November 14, 2005, from http://www.ciera.org/library/reports/inquiry-2/2-016/2-016h.html

Index

CORWIN
PRESS

The Corwin Press logo—a raven striding across an open book—represents the union of courage and learning. Corwin Press is committed to improving education for all learners by publishing books and other professional development resources for those serving the field of PreK–12 education. By providing practical, hands-on materials, Corwin Press continues to carry out the promise of its motto: **"Helping Educators Do Their Work Better."**

The National Association of Secondary School Principals—promoting excellence in school leadership since 1916—provides its members the professional resources to serve as visionary leaders. NASSP further promotes student leadership development through its sponsorship of the National Honor Society®, the National Junior Honor Society®, and the National Association of Student Councils®. For more information, visit www.principals.org.